The Secret Place

(formerly The Hide-Out)

Dorothy Webb

Illustrated by Donald Grey

Scripture Union
130 City Road, London EC1V 2NJ

Other books by Dorothy Webb:
Strangers in Trefoil Street

Reprinted 1971, 1974
Reissued as THE SECRET PLACE 1978
Reprinted 1978
Reprinted 1981

ISBN 0 85421 615 4

Printed and bound in Great Britain by
William Clowes (Beccles) Limited, Beccles and London

CHAPTER 1

Josie was leaning on a wall at the end of the street and watching a group of kids outside one of the houses. There were five of them. There was a playground for them at the Council block and it had five swings, two roundabouts and a dented slide, but none of the kids wanted to play there. So they were all standing around outside Jackie's house. Josie had followed them there.

Jackie was sitting on the wall of her house, swinging her legs. She was very important because she lived in a house, and she knew the other four were dying to be asked in. They lived in the Council flats. So they liked the stairs inside the house and they liked the back-yard.

Josie leaned and unconsciously swung one of her feet the way Jackie was swinging hers; the large bedroom slipper she was wearing fell off immediately, and she had to stoop to put it on again. While she was doing this, one of the girls noticed her.

"Look, there's Josie. What's she doing round here?"

"Nothing," said one of the boys. "She never does nothing."

Josie stood up, and saw them all looking at her. She pretended she was going along the street on an errand for her mum. She began to shuffle along in the bedroom slippers (which really belonged to her mum), trying to give a lighthearted little skip here and there as she'd seen other children do, coming home from school. The group round Jackie were across the road from her, but as she got level with them, the same girl who had noticed her before called out:

"Here, Josie! Where are you going?"

Josie didn't take any notice, and Anita shouted her question louder.

"Don't bother with her," said Jackie. "She never talks to no one, and she can't do nothing. Let's go to the playground."

Something inside took hold of Josie, and she stopped and called out, "I'm going shopping."

"Shopping?" asked the third girl, Sharon, derisively. "Where's your bag then?"

"Yeah!" shouted Anita. "Where's your bag and where's your money?"

Josie stared at them with her mouth open.

"Aw, come on," said Jackie, suddenly disgusted. "Leave her alone. I told you she can't do nothing."

Jackie had jumped off the wall, and the five children walked away towards the block of flats in which Anita lived, leaving Josie standing in the street, still trying to think of an answer to their jeers. They went to the playground and amused themselves for a while on the swings and the dented slide. But, after a while, some big boys came along and began to spoil their fun. They pushed the roundabout round too fast, blocked the slide by climbing up it, and began to take over all the swings. They each took two swings at a time, sitting on one and swinging the other with their hands.

Anita called Jackie over to one corner of the playground. "I'll ask my mum if you can stay to tea if you like," she offered.

"All right," said Jackie, "let's go and ask now. It's no fun here."

Anita's mother, high up on the fifth floor, looked down at her niece consideringly.

"What?" she said. "You her again? Don't I see enough of you?"

Jackie looked up at her and waited. She knew Auntie Marge always talked like this and never meant it. Anita said, "Can Jackie come to tea, mum?"

Auntie Marge looked consideringly again. Jackie was small and plump and cosy. She squashed down a smile at the corners of her mouth, and gazed up at her aunt, half laughing, half pleading.

"Go on, the pair of you," said Auntie Marge, roughly, and her hard hand tousled up all Jackie's cropped hair.

Anita and Jackie knew the battle was won.

She always spoke roughly, but she had a heart of gold, Jackie knew. Jackie's mum said so. Jackie was a little afraid of Auntie Marge's roughness sometimes, but not really ever afraid that Auntie Marge would say "no" to the things they wanted to do. Jackie's mum said "no" quite often. She was small and cosy, a grown-up version of Jackie, and she was quieter than Auntie Marge, but she often said "no". Auntie Marge never did.

Anita was spoilt. That was another thing Jackie's mum said. It was because she was the youngest, of course. Anita had four brothers and one sister. The next one up from Anita was Frankie, and he was quite grown-up, being seventeen. The others were still older and two of them were married. Anita would be eleven on November 5th, and she was an auntie already.

Jackie couldn't imagine what this felt like. She herself was the eldest and so was not spoilt, of course, especially as her mum said "no" so often. She had a brother, Colin, who was eight, and a little sister, Lindy, who was three and a half.

Besides all this, Anita must be spoilt because she was so pretty. She had big brown eyes and light brown hair which flowed down her back. She was always having new dresses, and her big sister, Irene, gave her all her cast-off bits of jewellery. Anita was always coming to school with new ear-rings and bracelets and necklaces, and last week Frankie had given her some money to buy a ring at the market.

With all these privileges, Anita got the best parts whenever the children did a play. Last Christmas she had been Mary in the Nativity at Church, and she was usually the princess, too, and wore one of Irene's dance dresses. Jackie was much cleverer than Anita, so she was always given parts with lots of speaking. Very often she had to be a man. She had been the most talkative shepherd in the Nativity. But she felt life was unfair.

For all this, she was fond of her cousin, and they spent a lot of out-of-school time together. This term they were going to be in the same class at school, although Jackie was a year younger than Anita. Mark and Sharon and Billy were going to be in their class, too, and so was Josie, though none of the children could understand how she'd got into Class One, when she couldn't read or write.

"I hope Miss lets us two sit together," said Anita, as they came down the steps to the bottom of the block, on their way back to Jackie's house to tell her mum.

"She's very strict though, won't let you talk—she was always telling me off last year," she added.

"You talk too much, that's why," said Jackie. "'Listen more and talk less'—that's what Miss Roberts was always saying to us."

"I don't talk," began Anita, loud and complaining. "I hardly say anything—she just picks on——"

She stopped suddenly. They had come out of the entrance to the flats by now, and Jackie looked where Anita was looking.

Josie had come shuffling back into the playground. She was a tall, thin girl, with a pale face and listless hair cut short by someone who didn't care much. Anita had stopped speaking, because one of the big boys, who now had the whole playground to themselves, was walking towards Josie swinging a rope from one hand.

"Get out of here! Get out of here!" he shouted.

Josie stood still and stared at him without saying anything. Jackie remembered afterwards, thinking that if it had been her she'd have turned round and run. But Josie evidently knew the boy, for he was calling her by her name and a lot of other names, too. The boy came right up and began swinging his rope at Josie, making it whistle just past her shoulders and across the top of her head. He was calling her ugly names and words which Jackie's mum had forbidden her to use, though Jackie had heard Auntie Marge and Uncle Sid and all her boy cousins using them sometimes.

"Who's that boy?" she whispered to Anita.

"It's Larry O'Dare," whispered Anita. "He lives in our block—on Josie's landing. I'm not going near him—he's horrible."

"He's going to hit her in a minute," said Jackie. "Oh, why don't she run away?"

"She's stupid, that's why," said Anita, scornfully. "Besides, she's used to being hit, she don't feel it, her dad's always hitting her."

"I'd run away," said Jackie. "Oh, what shall we do?"

The big boy was swinging the rope even nearer. Josie seemed to be paralysed. Another of the boys was creeping up from behind.

"That boy don't live here," said Anita. "We could get the porter, I suppose. He'd send them away."

But before they had time to do anything, the boy behind Josie made a sudden grab at her shoulders. Josie was taken by surprise, screamed in terror and jerked away, straight into the lashing rope.

The boy dropped his rope and roared with laughter, so did the other four. Josie had found the power of movement and now fled, straight towards the porch where the cousins were standing. They had one horrified look into the pale face with the scarlet weal, already swelling up, before Josie pushed past them and up the stairs.

"Josie," called Jackie, "you've dropped your slipper." But the child didn't stop, and they heard the sobs begin and echo down the stone steps, till they judged that she was waiting on the landing of the third floor to be let into her mother's flat.

"We'd better take her slipper up," said Jackie. She felt she must do something. "We should've got the porter to chase them boys away."

Anita, too, was feeling uncomfortable.

"Well, all right," she said, "come on."

As they went up the stairs they heard the door on the third floor open, and a hard woman's voice telling Josie to get on in and stop making such a row.

"Is that her mum?" asked Jackie. Anita said it was. "Cor, my mum wouldn't talk like that if I came home crying," said Jackie.

"No more would mine," replied Anita. "She'd give me sweets."

At the door they stopped. They could hear a din going on behind it. Josie was howling and sobbing, and her mum's voice could be heard above those of a number of children.

"Sounds like a monkey house," said Anita. "Go on, *you* knock."

Jackie knocked very loudly, and after a moment or two the woman came to the door, still shouting. She was tall, bony, dirty and untidy; yellow bleached hair hung in rats tails round her face, and a cigarette seemed to be stuck on her lower lip. When she opened the door, she did not look at Anita and Jackie at first, but turned back towards two filthy little boys in ragged trousers who were coming after her, grinning cheekily.

"Get back in there!" she screamed at them, and Jackie and Anita looked at each other, wrinkling up their noses. The woman smelt, and so did the flat. Then Josie's mum turned back to them.

"Josie dropped this," said Jackie politely, holding out the slipper. "And we've brought——" She didn't have a chance to finish. Josie's mum seized the slipper, as if Jackie had been trying to take it away, and slammed the door. The girls stared at one another.

"Well, if that's all the thanks we get," said Anita.

"That's the last time I pick up anything *she's* dropped," said Jackie, her cheeks going red with humiliation. They marched down the stairs. In the playground the boys were once again crawling all over the slide. They were trying to wrench one of the side pieces off near the top.

"No wonder they were hitting her," said Anita, on the boys' side now. "She deserved it—if she's like her mum."

Jackie, though angry, was more moderate.

"Well, she can't help her mum, can she?" she said after a bit. "I'm glad my mum ain't like hers."

"Mine ain't, either," said Anita, "but Josie's like her mum, I expect."

They went on for a bit in silence, and then Jackie, calming down a bit more, remarked, "We should've been and got the porter, Anita, just the same."

Anita said nothing. She felt ashamed of the way she'd stood by and done nothing when Josie was being bullied, but she thought they'd made up for it by taking the slipper back. She thought of Josie's mum and scowled.

"She ain't like her mum really," said Jackie. "She never said anything in our class last year. She'd never shout and screech like her mum did just now."

Still Anita scowled, but began to feel uncomfortable.

"And I don't think her mum is kind to her," said Jackie. This made Anita angry.

"Her dad ain't really her dad," she said suddenly. "My mum said so. She said that's why he hates her, and I think," she added, suddenly seeing a picture in her mind, "if them boys'd been hitting *us*, she wouldn't have gone to fetch the porter neither."

CHAPTER 2

Anita sat at her desk, with her elbows on it and her cheeks on her fists, and scowled. Jackie, sitting at the other side of the classroom, beside Mark, looked across at her cousin and smiled wickedly. Anita caught her eye and scowled even more bitterly. It was the first day back at school, and Miss Lawson had put her on the other side of the room from her cousin, and there was an empty place beside her. And she had specially asked to sit by Jackie! Miss Lawson had let her sit by Jackie for the first half hour of the morning. Then she had suddenly rearranged the whole room, and put her right on the other side, and had put Mark beside Jackie. She, Anita, had no one sitting beside her. Just because Miss Lawson had it in for her, and said she talked too much and never listened.

Anita was not listening now. She sat and brooded. Miss Lawson was explaining about teams and team-points, and of course Anita had heard it all before, because she had been in this class last year as well. She sat and brooded on her wrongs. Miss Lawson had it in for her, of course. She never let Anita give out pens and pencils or paper or books. This morning, being the first day of term, all these things had been given out, and Anita had not been chosen once. And when she had lost her rubber, Miss Lawson had just said curtly, "Find it." That was a lot of help, thought Anita. She would certainly never have found her rubber at all if she had not been made to change desks. The rubber had then turned up, underneath all the books she'd had to move. She would have had to do without a rubber for the whole term, thought Anita, glowering, for all Miss Lawson cared.

It was certainly not her day. Because she hadn't been listening, she put Jackie's name down when the time came to vote for team leaders, and was ridiculed before the whole class as a result.

"Have we a 'Jackie' amongst the Fourth Years?" asked Miss Lawson, in a pretending, surprised voice.

"No, Miss," chorused the class, enjoying seeing Anita going slowly red.

"And you know you don't have a 'Third Year' as a team leader," said Miss Lawson. "I told you that before, and you, of all people, should know Jackie's a 'Third Year'. Really, Anita, I am fast losing patience with you. You can't even listen when you're sitting right under my nose! Well, that's one vote wasted." She tore Anita's strip of paper in half, and tossed it into the waste-paper basket.

"Now, who are the team leaders?"

The names were read out. Kevin had been voted team leader for Red (Anita and Jackie's team); Janet was leader of Blue ("Of course," thought Anita. Janet was always being picked for things); Susan was leader of Yellow, and a boy called Robert was Green team leader. The deputy leaders were the people with the next largest number of votes. Anita wasn't even a deputy leader. She finished the morning in a dull and angry mood.

"Coming to Bible Club?" asked Jackie, cheerfully, in the dinner queue. Anita made a sniffing sort of grunt, and Jackie didn't know whether she was saying "yes" or "no".

"Come on," said Kevin, coming up behind them with his plate, "it's going to be good—it's a missionary."

Anita softened a bit, not because it was going to be a missionary, but because Kevin was talking to her as if she was just an ordinary member of the class and not the one who had been picked out for disgrace the whole morning. Jackie was relieved to notice a slight lifting of the scowl, and so she talked eagerly back to Kevin, and they all went and sat at the same table, talking loudly and eating fast.

"Who else is in our team, Kevin?" asked Jackie, when they were at the stodgy pudding stage. "I'm glad I'm in Red, I've been in Red team all through the school."

"Good team," said Kevin, casually. "There's ten of us in Class One, you and Anita, Mark, Marissa, Bernice—um—Alfred, Tommy, and oh, Les and me, of course—how many's that?"

"Nine," said Jackie, who had been counting on her fingers.

"One more," said Kevin. "Who can that be? Oh, I know—that Josie girl, who came up with your lot."

"Oh!" said Jackie and Anita in a disgusted chorus. Anita was glad to find another candidate for disgrace.

"She ain't no good. Where is she, anyway?"

"Not in school," said Kevin. "P'raps she's ill."

"Oh, she ain't ill," said Jackie, "she's just always being away, that's all. She was away half the time last year. That's why she ain't no good—can't read nor write, and she's a Fourth Year really."

"Coo!" said Anita, who didn't know as much about Josie's school work as her cousin. "Coo! How old is she then?"

"Ten," said Jackie, "least, she was ten last year; maybe she's eleven now."

"We'll have to get her to come every day," said Kevin, frowning. "Miss Lawson gives points to the best team for attendance."

"Oh, yes," said Anita. (She had quite forgotten her sulks now; besides, she herself was good at coming to school regularly.) "We can't have her spoiling things. Red had the attendance prize in Class One last year."

"Where does she live?" asked Kevin.

"Same block as me," said Anita, "but not the same landing." She was about to tell him the story of the bullies and the slipper and Josie's mum, but Kevin looked at the clock and stood up. "Hurry up," he said, "they'll be starting."

Anita hastily swallowed a last mouthful and rushed after the others. She still hoped to get a word in about the incident of Josie's slipper, but there was no chance. Miss Roberts and the missionary were going into the library as Kevin, Jackie and Anita came up. They squeezed into the crowded room and sat down as quickly as possible.

The missionary was young, and had a guitar. She sang to the children and taught them a chorus, then she put her guitar down on the table and told a story.

Far away in Vietnam, she said, lived a girl called Thoa. There was a war going on in her country and, when she was quite small, bombs had fallen on her village. Her mother and father, and all her brothers and sisters, had been killed in the bombing. Somehow

Thoa had escaped, but there was no one to look after her except some distant relations. They were so poor that they did not welcome the little girl but made her work very, very hard. She had no chance to go to school and learn things, but worked day after day on the little bit of land which belonged to her cousins. After a time she became ill, and soon everyone could see that she was suffering from leprosy. One day she fell and broke her foot, but because of the leprosy she could not feel anything. She did not dare stop working in case her cousins made her leave their home, so she went on hobbling about on the side of her foot and made it very much worse. Then a bomb fell into their little plot of ground and their home, and there was nowhere for Thoa and her cousins to live. They began to walk to the next village, but Thoa's injured foot held them all back. Then some soldiers came along in a lorry. They saw poor Thoa limping behind the others, and offered to take her to the hospital in the town. The cousins were only too glad to get rid of her, so the soldiers took her to the hospital, and then she was brought to the mission clinic to get better.

The missionary stopped suddenly, but the whole room was quiet, waiting for some more. Jackie's eyes had filled up with tears at the picture of the sick child tottering along the road behind the others. She took this opportunity to blink very hard. The missionary said, "The time's gone, I'm afraid, though there's a lot more I could have told you. To finish the story quickly, I'll just tell you that that little girl, Thoa, is living in our orphanage today. She helps the little ones who've only just been brought to us, and we really feel we couldn't do without her. She'll never be able to walk properly because she has only one foot now, but she has got very clever hands and she does a lot of sewing and needlework to help clothe the other children. And, most important of all, she's a real Christian. She told me herself that she'd never heard of the Lord Jesus Christ till she came to the clinic. But then she believed that what the nurse taught her about His love was true, because she saw that the nurse loved her enough to look after her when she needed it, although none of her own people had cared much."

After that, the missionary said a prayer, and then they all sang again to the guitar, and, because it was time to finish, most of the children went out, still singing, although Miss MacRae stopped strumming and put the guitar in its case. Jackie and Anita and some of the others lingered there.

"Were you there, Miss? When that little girl came in?" asked one of the boys.

"Yes," said Miss MacRae, "I look after the children

in the orphanage, so Thoa helps me a lot. I expect she'll have grown a lot bigger by the time I go back."

"When are you going back, Miss?" asked Anita.

"In the summer," replied Miss MacRae.

"Wish I could go out there, Miss," said Jackie, wanting this new person to notice her, too. "I'd like to help those poor people, I would."

"Yes, and me!" chorused several others immediately. Miss MacRae smiled gently and just a bit sadly. "You know, people suffering from leprosy are sometimes very ugly, and it's not much fun helping them."

"I wouldn't mind," said Jackie.

"After all," said someone else, "they can't help being ugly, can they?"

"Often they are stupid," went on Miss MacRae, deliberately. "You give them medicine to help them get better, and they do the wrong things with it—take it all in one go, instead of three times a day for a fortnight! Sometimes they sell it to someone else. I've often felt very angry about things like that."

"Miss Roberts says I'm stupid," said Mark, unconsciously. He had been thinking out loud, but everyone laughed and he went red and laughed, too.

"But, Miss," said Sharon loudly, above the laughter, "why do you help them then? They don't deserve it, if they're stupid like that."

Miss MacRae waited till the laughter had gone, then she said, "I do it because the Lord Jesus told me to, and sent me to Vietnam because He loves them, even when they're ugly and stupid."

The bell went, as a warning that afternoon school would start in five minutes.

"We'll talk about it a bit more in Bible Club next

Monday, if you like," said Miss Roberts. "Off you go now, all of you. Miss MacRae has a train to catch."

Still Jackie lingered, and Anita waited for her.

"Miss, I'd still like to go," said Jackie. "I'm a Christian, too. Miss Roberts knows."

"So am I," butted in Anita.

"Well," said Miss MacRae, "then the Lord Jesus has got some kind of job for you to do right here in Poplar, I expect."

"What sort of thing, Miss? There ain't no one with that leprosy here in Poplar," they said, following her to the library door.

Miss MacRae stopped and turned back to them. "Well, maybe you know someone that nobody wants —p'raps another boy or girl in your class. Maybe there's someone *you* know who is ugly and stupid, you think. Maybe you could love that boy or girl for Jesus's sake. If you did you'd be doing what we are trying to do in Vietnam. They don't *have* to have leprosy, you see. Now I must go. Goodbye."

She smiled again and went off down the corridor, watched by two astonished faces.

"Cor! I don't get that," said Anita.

CHAPTER 3

Josie was in her hide-out. She had not gone back to school on that first day of term, nor the second, nor even the third. It was now the fourth day, Friday.

Her hide-out was down by the wharves. Josie had discovered it one day when she had run away from her dad and his shouts and his belt. She'd come running up a street where there was nothing but a great high wall and a wood-and-iron gate right across the road. So she'd turned to see if she could climb the wall, because she was afraid of her dad coming after her. With her long bony legs and arms, she had discovered footholds in the lowest part of the wall, and struggled and heaved herself to the top. Once there, she had sat astride and seen, a long way below, a narrow bit of dusty yard, hemmed in by warehouses. The end of one warehouse was part of the wall Josie was sitting on. So she had not had much difficulty in climbing on to its roof and wriggling along it to the end. At the other end, she had discovered that she could not climb down, because the ground sloped away beneath the brick wall of the warehouse. But she had sat on the roof and gazed and gazed at the new sight, forgetting all about her dad. What she saw was the river—black and sluggish, moving between muddy banks and the green shiny sides of the wharves. Huge logs lay piled criss-cross everywhere on the wharves, and a great building had "Crown Saw Mills" written on it in very large letters (only Josie couldn't read the words). There had been nobody about, and the roof had been very uncomfortable with the sun beating down upon it. Also Josie had suddenly remembered that she might be seen from the road, so she had found a way of getting inside the warehouse. She had spotted the open window of the warehouse, looking out into the dusty bit of yard at the side. It had been a bit of a manoeuvre getting in. But she had managed it by lying on her stomach and dangling her skinny legs over the roof, and lowering herself bit by bit, until her feet reached the top of the open window frame. Then she had lowered and wriggled still more, holding on to the slates of the roof until her legs were inside the room and she was sitting on the window frame. After that, it had been quite easy to slide right in and drop down on to the dusty floor.

The room inside the warehouse was unused. It was bare except for a pile of sacking and some pieces of wood, but it had another window that faced on to the wharf, and it was this that had endeared it to Josie. There was nothing much to do there except kneel on a piece of sacking and peer out through the grime. Josie had spent the best part of four days doing just this. And they had been the happiest four days of her life. There was a lot to watch through the window; people were very busy on the wharves, loading and unloading things. Josie didn't bother to think about what the "things" were. She just watched the cranes going up and down, making criss-cross patterns against the hazy blue sky.

Nobody used her warehouse, and nobody saw the grimy face behind the cobwebs. So there was nobody there to hit her, or shout at her, nobody to laugh and jeer at her, nobody to ignore her because she wasn't fit to play with. It was all peace and quiet inside the hide-out. Only hunger drove her out at all.

* * * * *

It was September, and the evenings were still long and light. Quite suddenly the skipping season had arrived, and around every corner there were girls to be seen on the litter-strewn pavements, leaping and whirling ropes as if their lives depended on it. Jackie and Anita could hardly wait to get home from school and find themselves a piece of rope, or beg the money from their mothers to run to the shop and buy a proper skipping rope with coloured handles. They parted at the corner, and agreed to meet again in ten minutes with their ropes.

Jackie was happy. She raced down the street to her house, with the shouts of the skippers blowing past her in the dusty warm air. Lindy saw her coming and came trotting out of the gateway to meet her.

"Go on back! I'm going skipping, you can't come."

Lindy began to cry, noisy and unashamed. She had been waiting for Jackie all afternoon, because her mother had promised her that Jackie would take her to the swings. She was hot and grubby and tired of playing by herself in the tiny backyard, and she loved swinging more than anything. She trotted in to the house after Jackie, howling with her mouth as wide open as it would go.

"Aw, mum, tell her to go and play by herself," begged Jackie. "I want a piece of rope to go skipping with 'Nita."

"Oh!" said Jackie's mother, Mrs. Smith, disappointed. "I've promised our Lindy you'd take her on the swing. Be a sport, Jackie love, and take her. She's been waiting the whole afternoon."

"Oh, I can't," pouted Jackie, "I want a rope. I'm going skipping with 'Nita. Lindy'll get in the way."

"Well, I'm not finding you a rope unless you promise to take Lindy on the swing."

"But I'll have to push her all the time," complained Jackie. "She can't jerk herself; I'll have to stand there pushing, and I'll never get any skipping done."

"When you've given her a swing, you can bring her back and go and skip as much as you like," said Mrs. Smith, firmly. "Anyway, if you take her now, I'll look for a rope and have it waiting for you when you come back."

Jackie saw she was beaten and turned to take Lindy's hand. Lindy gave her a beaming smile, the tears still rolling down her cheeks and making clean marks down her grubby face.

"Look at her," said Jackie, disgustedly, "she wants her face washed."

"That won't take a minute," said Mrs. Smith, passing over a convenient flannel. "And give her a proper, decent swing, mind. You won't have your rope for another ten minutes." Then she turned back to her ironing.

Jackie wiped Lindy's face and took her out and down the street. Anita was at the corner but she had no rope. Anita began calling out as soon as she saw her cousin, "Jackie, I'm not coming skipping after all, I'm going for a ride on Frankie's motor-bike, Ta-Ta!"

She didn't even wait for Jackie and Lindy to come

up to her, but raced across the road and around the corner. Jackie could hear the engine revving up, and she dragged Lindy up to the corner just in time to see Frankie, in his black leather motor-bike outfit and his crash helmet and goggles, pushing off from the kerb and turning in a wide sweep, with the excited Anita clutching him and looking back to see if her cousin could see her. Then they were off with a roar and a splutter and around the next corner, at a terrific speed.

"Oh, well," thought Jackie, "s'pose she'll be back by the time I've given Lindy a swing." But she pushed Lindy back and forth for what seemed like hours in the playground belonging to the Council flats, and still there was no sign of the motor-bike or of Frankie or Anita. Every time Jackie heard an engine roaring she stopped pushing and looked up, but every time it was someone else in black leather, with a crash helmet with goggling eyes painted on the back of it, roaring round the block.

There were hardly any children in the playground. Once Josie came through it. She shuffled along in her huge bedroom slippers with her eyes on the dusty ground. Jackie would not have bothered to speak, only she was so bored. She stopped pushing again, and sat on the swing next to Lindy's, pushing herself off with her feet and trying to swing in time with Lindy so she could hold her swing, too.

"Hi, Josie," she called. "Where you been? We was at school all this week and you wasn't there."

Josie looked at her but didn't reply. Then she looked at Lindy. She stopped shuffling and stared. Lindy was a pretty child with short dark curls, and dark eyes with curling eyelashes. Now that her face had been tidied up, it could be seen to be a glowing peachy colour, and she was humming dreamily to herself as she swung to and fro.

Josie just stood and stared at Lindy. She looked like a fish, thought Jackie, contemptuously, with goggling eyes and half-open mouth. She decided that it was time she and Lindy went home. The sun had disappeared and the blocks and the cranes and the gas-tower were showing darker than ever, against a deepening sky with a touch of pink.

"Come on, we're going now."

Josie found her voice. "Who's she?"

"She's my sister. Who do you think she is?"

Josie stared after them as they marched away down the street. Something she couldn't express was welling up in her, and she longed to pick Lindy up and hug her. She would willingly have pushed her on the swing for hours. She watched the two stout little figures going hand in hand until they got right up to Jackie's house and went in, without looking back. Her envy of Jackie was complete.

Jackie had a curious dream that night. She was in a funny sort of room, and Lindy was there and a whole lot of other people. The place had stone walls and bars on the windows and there was only one door, which was shut tight. All the people were walking around, and Lindy was tugging at her arm and howling. Suddenly a woman in a blue dress rushed up and said very crossly, "What are you making that child cry for? Why don't you take her on the swings?" And before Jackie could answer, she had picked up Lindy and darted out of the little door, slamming it behind her. Jackie felt very worried because she'd lost Lindy, and she tried to get out of the door and it wouldn't open. Then suddenly Mr. Humphreys, the Headmaster of St. Barnabas, was standing in front of the door, stopping her. He said, "I've told you before, young lady, you don't go out of this door on your own. You've got to have somebody with you." Jackie looked round desperately, and there, staring at her with goggle eyes and slack mouth, was Josie Pugsey. And, at that moment, the bubble burst and she was awake, staring at a flower on the wallpaper, and Lindy was poking her in the back and shouting.

It was Saturday morning, as it happened, and later that morning Anita called for Jackie to come shopping in the market. This was a favourite Saturday morning occupation for them, which their mothers encouraged, providing them with large shopping bags and lists to match. On their way, Anita told Jackie about her motor-bike ride and Jackie told Anita about her dream.

"Ugh!" said Anita. "Fancy dreaming about Josie Pugsey! What a nightmare!"

"I know, it was," said Jackie. "She ain't half ugly."

Then a thought struck her. "You know that little girl what had leprosy what that lady told us about in school?"

"Yes," said Anita.

"Well, she might have been ugly, mightn't she?"

"Yes, she was," said Anita, positively, "the missionary said so."

"Well, she turned out all right in the end, didn't she? And that lady had to put up with her while she was getting better."

"Yes," said Anita, considering. "Missionaries have to put up with things, don't they?"

"She told us——" said Jackie, doggedly. "She told us *we* could do it, too. Don't you remember?"

Anita walked along blankly. Jackie had really got going now.

"We could make friends with Josie Pugsey, d'you see? And maybe she'd get better and better, I mean nicer'n nicer. She ain't got no friends at all."

Anita stopped still and turned round in the street and stared at Jackie.

"Cor!" she said. "You're nuts! You must be joking!"

CHAPTER 4

Just the same, it was Anita who started the whole thing off. She met Josie dawdling downstairs from the third floor, in good time for school, on the following Tuesday morning. Anita had a new dress on and was carrying a satchel. She wanted someone to admire it.

"Hullo! You coming to school?"

Josie's mouth opened and shut, a habit she had instead of talking. She went down the rest of the stairs beside Anita and looked sideways at the satchel and new dress. A longing welled right up inside her for the things Anita had, and she began to hate Anita. She wanted to say some spiteful things—that Anita's dress was awful, that she was a show-off, that her satchel was horrible. But she was too afraid to say any of them.

Outside the door, at the bottom of the stairs, Jackie was waiting with her skipping rope in her hand. As soon as Anita saw her cousin, she began opening her satchel and getting out a beautiful rope. It was brand new, creamy-coloured, and it had yellow wooden handles.

"Cor!" said Jackie, looking at her old rope in disgust. "My mum wouldn't let me have a new one."

"My mum wouldn't neither," said Anita, "but I started to cry and Frankie gave me the money."

"Cor!" said Jackie again, thinking enviously how she would like to be spoilt like that.

"Come on, let's skip."

Anita set off across the playground. Just then Jackie noticed Josie. She decided now was her chance.

"Hullo, Josie," she said, a bit self-consciously. Josie's mouth opened and shut.

"Coming to school?" said Jackie. Josie had not gone to school on Monday because no one in their flat had got up in time, so she had stayed in the hide-out all day on her own instead. But this morning her mother had got up and pushed her and her two brothers out of the door of the flat. The two little boys had gone running off somewhere. Josie had been going to go to her hide-out again. Now she changed her mind. She would go to school with Jackie, so she nodded.

"Aw, come on, Jackie," called Anita from across the playground. "Ain't you gonna skip?"

Jackie glanced at Josie's feet and saw she had her mother's shoes on again. She decided that she would stay with Josie and talk to her, and see if Josie would get a bit better. She started walking across the playground, and Josie shuffled at her side. Anita skipped back towards them and stopped only a few yards away.

"Ain't you gonna skip?" asked Anita, yet again, with a "getting ready to sulk" look in her eye.

"No, don't let's skip," said Jackie. "Josie ain't got no rope." She felt rather pleased with herself after saying that, because there was nothing Anita could say without looking very mean indeed.

The three of them walked to school in silence. Anita sulked and said nothing. She did not, in fact, cheer up until they were nearly at St. Barnabas, and then Sharon came round the corner and began to admire her satchel and rope and dress. Josie did not say a word the whole way either. Jackie could not think of anything to say to either of them, and she got rather fed up and began to wish she had skipped after all, and left Josie behind.

They walked up the East India Dock Road and picked out a certain green petrol lorry which was stuck in among the others in the traffic jam, and wondered if they could race it to the Blackwall Tunnel. They nearly did, too, only Josie walked out of one of her mum's shoes and had to go back and get it.

Jackie had time to think, anyway, and she decided it would be more fun making friends with Josie if Josie were provided with a skipping rope and a pair of the right size shoes. She thought she would get Josie to skip during playtime, and tell her to get her mum to give her a rope and buy her a pair of plimsolls. So when playtime came she went up to Josie and said, "Come on and skip."

Anita did not like the idea at first, but later on she got interested in Josie's efforts, in spite of herself, and began to try and help. Josie was certainly not very good at skipping. Her arms and legs did not seem to work together, so that she jumped up in the air while the rope was flying over her head and landed with a thump just as it was passing under her feet. She could not seem to get the right rhythm. Jackie tried hard to be kind and encouraging when the bell went.

"You'll have to practise a bit, then you'll get it. Your jumping's not bad. Get your mum to give you a piece of clothes line."

Josie stared blankly, then she said, "Yes, I'll get a rope from my mum."

She spoke so rarely that her voice was an astonishment. It was quite deep and powerful.

Afterwards, Anita had doubts about Josie's mum giving her a rope. "She never has nothing," said Anita. "I should know, she lives in our block."

"Well, p'raps we could get a rope for her," said Jackie, with a worried little frown. "P'raps we could find some plimsolls for her."

Mark was with them at the time. The three of them were tidying up in the Art Room after school.

"That Josie," said Mark, "I heard her singing in the corridor this afternoon. I never heard her singing before. Have you ever heard her sing?"

"No," said Anita, "never heard her speak, let alone sing."

"Do you think she's cheering up?" asked Jackie, suddenly.

"I dunno," said Mark, "but she sings all right."

"Maybe we could get her to be good at something," said Jackie. She felt encouraged to think that Josie had begun to improve already.

That night both she and Anita asked their mums if they had anything that would do for Josie. Auntie Marge found an old pair of plimsolls that had been Irene's, and Anita brought them to school in her satchel the next day to see if they would fit Josie. Jackie wheedled another old piece of clothes line from her mum and brought that.

The plimsolls did fit Josie—well, better than her other shoes had, at any rate. But Jackie need not have bothered about the clothes line, for Josie turned up at school the very next morning with a lovely skipping rope with red and yellow handles. It looked new.

"Where did you get that?" asked Anita. "Did you have one at home all the time?"

"No," said Josie, a bit sullenly, "I bought it down the shop yesterday."

"But it's not new, is it?" asked Anita. "It's nearly new, but look at that long scratch on the handle. You wouldn't have done that to it already if you only bought it yesterday."

"I bought it," said Josie, "it's mine. I bought it yesterday, down the shop."

She began to try to skip across the playground. Anita turned to Jackie and Mark.

"I don't think she's telling the truth. I seen that rope somewhere before."

The more she thought about it, the more convinced she became. Then suddenly the truth dawned on her —unfortunately it was in the middle of geography, and she could not reach Jackie to tell her, and had to keep it in till the bell rang at afternoon play.

"That skipping rope is Susan Bates' in Class Four," she said, as soon as she got near Jackie. Jackie wouldn't believe her.

"She said she bought it. You're saying she's a liar."

"Well, Susan Bates got one exactly like that, and she lives on Josie's landing."

"Well, they probably sell them down the shop like Josie said," said Jackie, defensively, watching Josie stumble across the playground, tripping over her rope twice as many times as she jumped it.

"Ask Susan Bates," said Anita, fiercely.

"All right," said Jackie, just as fiercely. The two marched side by side across the playground without speaking. Each was quite sure that she was right.

Susan Bates was a round-faced, fair-haired child of seven. She was playing "Mothers and Fathers" with some of her closest friends in the corner near the shelter. The cousins marched determinedly up and cornered her.

"Susan," began Anita, who knew her best, "what you done with your skipping rope?"

Susan looked at Anita scornfully.

"I lost it, you know that. I lost it—you was helping me look for it last night."

"Yes, I know," said Anita, "but Jackie don't believe you lost it. Tell her where you lost it."

"Down in the playground outside the block," said Susan. "I left it on the floor and went and played on the swings and the slide, and when I come back it wasn't there."

Jackie faced Anita, and her cheeks began to go very red.

"You didn't tell me you *knew* she lost it."

"You didn't ask me," said Anita. "You didn't give me a chance to say."

"Anyway, that don't prove nothing," said Jackie. "How do you know Josie's is Susan's?"

"Well, ask her then," shouted Anita.

"All right, I will."

Jackie ran across to Josie. "Anita says your rope belongs to Susan Bates in Class Four," she puffed. "Come and tell her it don't."

Josie stared, and her mouth opened and shut. Then to Jackie's surprise she turned her back and began trying to skip away. Just then the bell went.

"What did she say?" asked Anita, coming up behind Jackie as she walked in to school.

"Nothing."

"I'm going to tell Miss."

There was nothing Jackie could do about it. Anita told Miss Lawson the accusation, and Miss Lawson sent for Susan from Class Four and asked her to describe the rope.

"Red and yellow handles," said Susan, importantly. "Nearly new. My mum bought it for me last week. There weren't nothing wrong with it only I scratched the handle." Anita, standing by Miss Lawson's desk, gasped.

"Josie's rope got a scratch on the handle, Miss," she said, loudly.

"Sit down, Anita. Now, Josie, have you got your rope here for me to see?"

Josie shook her head.

"Where is it?"

Josie's mouth opened and shut, then opened and

shut again. She was very pale. Miss Lawson spoke more kindly.

"I just want you to fetch your rope, Josie. I only want to look at it. We must clear this up, mustn't we? We can't have people saying other people are stealing things in our school."

Josie's mouth opened and shut again.

"Now I know you've got your skipping rope in school with you," said Miss Lawson, "be a sensible girl and fetch it. Is it in the cloakroom?"

Josie nodded.

"Go and fetch it then."

Josie went out of the room and the class waited. A long time passed and Miss Lawson suddenly got up.

"Take out your topic books and get on with topic work, quietly, please. Susan, come with me."

She took Susan by the hand and led her out of the room. They were not sure what happened outside, but after a time Mr. Humphreys came into the room with Miss Lawson and Susan. Josie was not with them. Mr. Humphreys went and opened Josie's desk. Anita saw the next bit clearly because, to her great disgust, Miss Lawson had given Josie the empty place next to her. The skipping rope lay in Josie's desk, under an exercise book. Mr. Humphreys removed it in silence, and once more he and Miss Lawson and Susan went out of the room. After that Miss Lawson came back alone and nothing was said. Josie did not come back into the classroom. But, when the bell went at the end of the afternoon and the children streamed out into the corridor, there stood Mrs. Bates and Susan and Mrs. Pugsey and Josie outside the Headmaster's room. Josie's eyes were as red and swollen as they could be.

CHAPTER 5

The next morning Josie was not in school, and Susan Bates was playing in the playground with a nearly new skipping rope with a scratch on one of the red and yellow handles. Anita had to enjoy her triumph on her own, however, because Jackie was much too angry to walk to school with her cousin.

"I'll never speak to Anita again," she had stormed to her mother that night, and true to this resolution she had not waited at the door of Anita's block the next morning. Anita felt very resentful. After all, she had been right and Jackie had been wrong. She poured it all out to Sharon and Mark and Billy.

"Jackie's stupid," said Sharon. "Everyone knows that Josie Pugsey ain't no good. What's Jackie so bothered about?"

Meanwhile, Jackie had never been in such a dreadful turmoil, and she didn't know what to do about it. She boiled inside when she saw Susan Bates with the skipping rope before school started. She boiled inside when she thought of Josie letting her down by stealing it. But most of all she boiled when she thought of Anita, and she was never going to speak to Anita again, ever.

After Assembly that morning, Mr. Humphreys came in and gave the whole of Class One a special talk.

"I'm talking to this class," he said, "because you're the top class and I want you all to try and help. Now you all know by now that Josie Pugsey stole a skipping rope, don't you?"

Everyone nodded violently.

"Stealing is wrong," said Mr. Humphreys, "always wrong, whatever reason you may have to steal. I want you to be very sure of that, for one thing. But I want you to know something else. Susan has got her skipping rope back and Josie has been punished. When Josie comes back to school, which will be tomorrow, I don't want anyone to say a word to her about it. She's had her punishment, and now we must forget it. This is very important. We must learn to forgive and forget. This is part of being a Christian."

He went out, and there was a bit of a buzz which Miss Lawson began to quell with the beginning of her arithmetic lesson. Jackie did not join in the buzz, however. She sat very still in her desk, and was conscious of Mr. Humphreys' words, "Forgive and forget". They soothed the part of her that was very hurt, deep inside. People did wrong things, she knew, but you weren't to give them up. She was going to go on being friends with Josie. Mr. Humphreys would have said it was right. And—and—maybe, even, she could be friends with Anita again—if Anita spoke first, of course.

That afternoon, when Class One was feeling drowsy after stodgy pudding and custard, Miss Lawson gave them a pleasant surprise.

"At half-term," she said, "Mr. Humphreys wants us to do an operetta on Parents' Evening."

Class One was very excited, though they hadn't even a vague idea what an operetta was.

"It's a story made with songs—a sort of musical," explained Miss Lawson. "We haven't a lot of time, but if everyone works hard and comes regularly we should be able to manage it. Of course, I won't be able to give a part to anyone who's away all the time, so it's up to you."

Everyone was to think of a story they would like the class to do, and tomorrow they would decide on one of them and begin to write the songs themselves. Jackie and Anita were so excited that they went home talking about it, and it was only when Jackie said, "Goodbye—see you tomorrow," at the corner of Anita's block, that she suddenly remembered she was speaking to Anita again, and she could not remember who it was who'd spoken first!

That evening Jackie watched a play on television. At first she just flopped into a chair in front of the set and watched contentedly, happy that everything had sorted itself out again. She was friends with Anita and she could be friends with Josie, and everything would be all right. Then an American soldier walked into the play she was watching, and someone said something about Vietnam. It was a grown-up play, and Jackie didn't know what it was all about, but it gave her a brilliant idea. Why couldn't their school operetta be about Thoa, from Vietnam? The boys could be soldiers and the girls could be nurses, and they could have Thoa and her family and a chorus of orphanage children. It would be just right for an operetta. She left Colin in charge of the television and rushed to tell her mother all about it. Mrs. Smith thought it was a very good idea.

"But don't you get too excited," she warned.

"Forty other kids in the class, *they* mightn't like the idea. I can think of one for a start."

"Who?" asked Jackie.

"Your cousin," said Mrs. Smith. "Anita likes to be the princess, don't she? And there ain't no princesses in that story."

"She can be Thoa," said Jackie, and remembered at once that Thoa was ugly and crippled. She began to have doubts about her idea. But another idea came at once. "No, I know! We could have Josie as Thoa."

"Josie?" said Mrs. Smith. "Is she that one that stole the skipping rope? Thought she wasn't never at school."

"No," said Jackie, slowly, "but she's ugly, *and* she can sing. Mark Billings said so."

Mrs. Smith began to laugh. "I shouldn't take what Mark Billings says! And it's the first time I ever heard you had to be ugly to get the best part."

Jackie had plenty of doubts after that, but the next day in school Miss Lawson asked for suggestions, and after "Cinderella" and "Sleeping Beauty" there was a pause. Jackie found her hand going up, tentatively.

"Please Miss, couldn't we do Thoa?"

"Thoa? What do you mean?"

Miss Lawson had forgotten the missionary's story, it seemed. There was some confusion while the Bible Club members rushed to explain. To Jackie's surprise and encouragement both Miss Lawson and the other children liked the idea a lot. Even Anita didn't object. Miss Lawson put the story on the board and they set to work with pencils and paper, to make a list of songs that would fit in at various points in the story. Kevin was very good at this.

"We could have a song for the soldiers to start

with, and then a song for the peasants," he said. It would be a war song for soldiers, but a sad song for peasants. Thoa would have to sing a verse by herself in the peasants' song, and then she and her relations would mime the first part of the story. Kevin also thought of a "Relations' Song" for Thoa's relations to sing, and Thoa would mime how she had hurt her foot. Then there would be a trekking song for the peasants and another soldiers' song. After that, Thoa would be brought to the missionaries and there would be a Mission Station song. (Anita suggested a hymn at this point, and Miss Lawson did not seem to think it a bad idea.)

Miss Lawson insisted that they should have the story and songs completely worked out before deciding who should take which part. Jackie heaved a sigh of relief, for Josie was not in school again that day.

"I dunno what you're bothering for," grumbled Anita, at playtime. "What do you want her to have a part for?"

"She don't deserve one—she never comes to school," butted in Sharon, who was listening. Jackie looked at Sharon with dislike.

"She can sing. Mark said he heard her singing," she said glaring. "And what's it got to do with you, anyway; I suppose you think *you* can be Thoa? That's a laugh!"

Sharon was furious. She said, "No, I don't. You can be Thoa, you're ugly enough."

A big fight might have followed, only Jackie suddenly felt ashamed of herself. She pressed her lips together tightly so she couldn't say anything else, and walked away. Anita followed her.

"Well, I don't care who's Thoa."

"I don't, I'm sure," said Sharon, somewhat taken aback at Jackie's letting her have the last word.

Josie and Thoa had somehow become mixed up in Jackie's mind. Jackie was quite sure that if only Josie were in school on The Day (that is, the day Miss Lawson gave out the parts for the operetta), she would immediately be given Thoa's part, it was obvious. Anita and Sharon, neither of whom were renowned for brains, just didn't see the point, as usual. The trouble was Jackie didn't know which day Miss Lawson would choose to give out the parts. She supposed the only thing to do was to get Josie along to school every day. This thought coincided with a discussion Red team had about getting top marks for attendance. Kevin said, disgustedly:

"We'd be all right if that Josie'd come."

"I knew she'd let us down," said Anita.

Kevin turned on her. "Well, *you'll* have to make her come to school then. You said she lived in your block."

"Here!" gasped Anita. "She don't live on my landing, and I'm not calling for her! Her mother's awful, ain't she, Jackie?"

But Jackie was deaf to the appeal. She had just learnt a verse in Bible Club, which kept popping up in her mind, "All things work together for good to them that love God." Now she was sure that Kevin's idea was one of the "things" working for her, so she could help Josie get the part. With this in her mind, she looked sweetly at Anita. "I know, I'll come and call for you every morning, and then we'll both go and call for Josie."

Anita had been horrified at the thought of going

alone, but Jackie's offer made everything all right. Between them, they would get Josie to school every day, and Red team would win Miss Lawson's attendance prize.

Jackie arranged to leave home five minutes earlier the next morning. Things did seem to be working together to help them. When they arrived at the third floor they found the door just opening and Josie's dad pushing her outside. The two children were afraid of Josie's dad. He was a bristly, snarling man, with a fearful temper. Apparently this morning he had decided Josie was to go to school, so that the attendance officer would not come round bothering him. So he was shoving Josie outside the door, very roughly, and threatening to march her all the way there if she didn't stop crying and start moving at once. Then he caught sight of Anita and Jackie, who were so petrified they were about to run back upstairs to Anita's flat.

"Here! You going to school?" he bawled. They nodded. "Well, take her with you, and mind she gets there."

He shoved Josie towards them. Still nodding violently to show that they had no thought of refusing, the two seized Josie's hands and began to drag her downstairs as quickly as they could.

For them, it was the first of many dreary walks to school. Josie hardly uttered a word for the whole of the first week, and she simply refused to skip, although Jackie brought the piece of washing line and offered it to her. She looked blank when they talked about the operetta. In fact, she never talked about anything.

At the beginning of the third week of the term, however, Mrs. Smith came to school with them because she wanted to talk to Mr. Humphreys about Colin's eyesight, and she brought Lindy in the push-chair. Jackie was so pleased about it that she nearly forgot to call for Anita. But Mrs. Smith reminded her, and promised to wait in the street while Jackie went up. Josie was waiting for them on her landing when they came down. When they got outside again, she gave them quite a shock.

"Aw! Your little sister!" she cried.

Jackie and Anita stared at her (as they always did whenever that big deep voice came out of Josie Pugsey's mouth), and they saw her face was one big smile at Lindy. They'd never seen Josie smiling before. She ran over to the push-chair and at once began talking and playing with Lindy. Mrs. Smith looked kindly down at the beaming face.

"How'd you like to push her, Josie?" she asked.

Josie's mouth opened and shut, but this time no

sound came out because of the rapture that was inside. She took the push-chair and pushed it slowly and proudly all the way to school. Jackie was almost going to grumble, because her mum hadn't let her have a push, but Mrs. Smith caught her eye and gave her a very hard look. And Jackie knew, deep inside, that Josie had been given this privilege because she had nothing else, and Jackie was satisfied. She and Anita skipped that morning. They skipped on ahead of the others, down the road by the Blackwall Tunnel, skipping up dust with their ropes and hitting pieces of litter aside. They turned back at the East India Dock Road, and skipped back to the others, and saw that Lindy was laughing at them and clapping her hands, and Josie was talking away to Mrs. Smith and Mrs. Smith was talking away to her and smiling down at her.

The sun was smiling away in the autumn sky, and there was a faint haze around the blocks. There was a haze of scaffolding around a great new block that was being put up, as well as the usual mistiness that always hangs in the sky over the East End. It was going to be a good day, thought Jackie. Here was Josie in school again after a whole week of regular attendance, and talking, too—nineteen to the dozen. She didn't look half so ugly when she beamed like that, either.

To crown everything, Miss Lawson said she was going to give out the operetta parts after prayers. Jackie felt that she had achieved everything. She did not care what part she had. She was not specially good at singing and expected to be put in the peasants' chorus. But Josie would be Thoa. Josie was next to Jackie in the hall, and she heard the deep voice singing heartily. Josie didn't know and couldn't read the words, but she was singing "la-la" and keeping in tune very well.

At last they were back in class, and Miss Lawson was standing with the list in her hands. Class One were sitting with their backs so straight and their arms so tightly folded that they all looked as if they had pains in the stomach—all except Billy, who had dropped his pencil and was crawling around on the floor looking for it. Miss Lawson waited, watching him. The class began to hiss and get impatient. At last, Les, who sat next to him, kicked him and he looked up and went pink under the thirty-nine pairs of impatient eyes. He scrambled on to his seat, making it scrape, and Miss Lawson winced.

She began to read the list. She started with the less important parts and kept "Thoa" till last. Sharon and Kevin were both missionaries, Janet was the missionary nurse who told Thoa about the Lord Jesus, Anita and Jackie were among Thoa's relations, Mark and Billy were soldiers—and "Thoa", said Miss Lawson, and paused, "will be Marissa".

CHAPTER 6

Marissa was one of those people who never lose any points for her team. What is more, her tall letters were very tall and her small ones always exactly the same size, so that her handwriting was always being held up as a model to the class. She had a clear, trilly little voice, and did not get shy about singing on her own, so she was clearly a very good choice for the part of Thoa. She even looked right, being rather small and thin, with a thick, oily plait and a light-brown skin.

Jackie sat hunched in her desk, frowning over at Marissa, who was looking pleased. The rest of the class was looking pleased, too, because, as well as the above-mentioned virtues, Marissa was not particularly clever. She was moderate in everything, so nobody was jealous of her. Indeed, if it hadn't been for her plan about Josie, Jackie would have been as pleased as everyone else that Marissa had got the part.

But what about Josie? Josie would be just—— Jackie suddenly straightened up—why, Josie didn't have a part at all! Miss Lawson hadn't read out her name. Well, something would have to be done about that, at once.

It was impossible to say anything till playtime, however. Jackie kept putting her hand up, but so did about twenty other people, all wanting to ask questions about the operetta—what clothes they would wear, when they would start practising the songs, when was it being done—until Miss Lawson decided to change the subject and have some peace. She set them all sums, with dire penalties for those who talked and didn't finish.

At last the bell went, and they were free. Jackie rushed up to Miss Lawson's desk and puffed anxiously.

"Please, Miss Lawson, you didn't give Josie a part in the play."

Miss Lawson looked blank for a moment. Her mind had been on other things, then she came back to earth again.

"Oh, Josie. Oh dear, didn't I? I suppose I forgot. Let me see now——" Her gaze wandered over to Josie, who was lingering by the door, waiting for Jackie. She had her bit of washing-line in her hand, and was mouthing some words at Jackie—something like, "Come on, hurry up, don't you want to skip?"

Miss Lawson looked startled, as if she had never realized that Josie could do more than nod or shake her head.

"Well, she can be a peasant," said Miss Lawson, looking for her list among the muddle of her desk. "That's easily put right."

"Oh, Miss," said Jackie, disappointed, "can't she be something better than that?"

"Well, er—I think we've got enough missionaries."

"I didn't mean that. I mean, can't she sing?"

"Well, everybody's going to sing, Jackie, don't be silly."

Miss Lawson found her list and put Josie's name down with the peasants.

"Go on out to play now, both of you."

It happened at this moment that Anita came back

to see why Jackie was so slow. She heard the last bit of the conversation, and said on an impulse, "Have you heard Josie singing, Miss? She got a nice voice."

Everyone looked surprised at this, including Josie. Miss Lawson was going out, but she hesitated at the bottom of the Staff Room stairs.

"Well, if Josie has a nice voice, we must hear her sing, and we can write in another part for her, but she'll have to come every day. No staying away or not turning up on Parents' Evening."

She went upstairs, and Anita and Jackie beamed at each other, and Josie stared. Then she spoke.

"Ain't you lot coming outside ever?"

In the playground they told some of the others. Mark and Kevin, Billy and Les had been playing football and had landed the ball into the yard next door. Billy had gone to Mr. Humphreys to ask if they could get it, and while the others were lounging around they heard the news from the girls. They were all very pleased that Josie might be given a part, and their pleasure infected Josie. Her cheeks became quite pink with excitement. Then she did seven skips in a row, without tripping. Jackie was delighted once more. She kept whispering inside herself, "She's getting better and better. Soon she'll be quite nice."

Miss Lawson kept her promise to hear Josie sing that afternoon. It was the day for the boys to go swimming, and the girls sometimes had netball with Miss Lawson. Today, however, she took them into the hall, and they tried out some of the songs they had made up for the operetta.

Marissa sang her solos, and was criticized because she could not be heard at the back of the hall, so she tried again. The first was a sad little verse from the peasants' song—the words were Janet's achievement—but Jackie thought Marissa could have acted a bit better while she was singing. She stood so stiffly and even smiled at one place. She felt sure Josie could have done better. The last song that Thoa was to sing, however, was a chorus, well known to all the St. Barnabas children, and it was much brighter and more cheerful. Marissa had to sing it on her own, and then the class joined in with her, everyone coming on stage as a sort of "grand finale". The girls practised this now. The chorus was a great favourite, and Jackie noticed that even Josie knew the words.

> The best for God, the best for God,
> I want to be the very, very best for God.
> It's the only thing worth being,
> It's the only life worth living,
> So I'll live it, and I'll be it, the best for God.

The tune was gay and, catching the excitement of the moment, the girls of Class One lifted up their heads and opened their mouths. Miss Lawson seemed very pleased with the sound that came out. When they'd finished she left the piano, smiling.

"That's fine. Now if you'll all come quietly down and sit on the floor, over here——" There was a general scuffle and the thing was achieved. "I want to hear Josie." Everybody murmured and looked at Josie, who stared at Miss Lawson. Jackie nudged her.

"Go on over! She wants you by the piano."

Josie still sat there. Miss Lawson struck an encouraging chord on the piano.

"Come along, now what can you sing to me?"

Still Josie did not move. Now everyone round about her was nudging her and telling her to get up and go over to the piano. It was Anita who did it in the end. She stood up, took hold of Josie's arm and pulled her. Josie got up and Anita led her over to the piano. Once there, Josie looked as if she was going to make a dash for the door. Anita stood grimly beside her.

"What do you want to sing to me, Josie?" said Miss Lawson again, in a trying-hard-to-be-kind voice. Josie, looking like a dying fish, stared, petrified and dumb. Anita looked over at Jackie, shrugging her shoulders and spreading out her hands to show she had done her best and could do no more.

"Oh," thought Jackie, "she *got* to sing now. Oh, please make her sing, she *got* to sing!"

A thought came back to her; that chorus, "The best for God", Josie knew that one.

"Make her sing 'Best for God' Miss," she called out hastily. "She knows that one."

"Yes," said Anita, quickly by the piano, "she sings that one all right, Miss."

"All right," said Miss Lawson, playing the opening bars, " 'The best for God'—ready, Josie?"

Miss Lawson played the note and began slowly, waiting for Josie's voice to come, but Josie was still dumb. Miss Lawson stopped, played the note and began the tune again. Jackie was nearly bursting with frustration. She wanted to leap up from the floor and *make* Josie sing. Anita was poking Josie.

"Go on, sing it. Go on."

The girls on the floor were sighing and looking at each other.

Sharon whispered loudly, "What a waste of time! *We* could be singing."

"She *can* sing, Miss," said Anita, desperately. "Honest, she can."

Miss Lawson looked over the piano top at her, and suddenly seemed to understand.

"Well, why don't you sing with her to start her off?" She started again, and Anita began singing loudly, "The best for God, the best for God . . ." The whole class joined in, "I want to be the very, very best for God." They sang it right through. But Josie did not sing one word. She was standing by the piano, looking down at her feet, looking miserable. Miss Lawson gave up.

"All right, Josie, if you don't want to sing, we won't make you. Go and sit down now," she said, quite kindly. Josie went and sat down, and Anita sat down also. The girls sang some more of the choruses and then the bell went for home-time.

Jackie was so fed up with Josie for letting her down.

She felt she just couldn't be bothered with her any more. There were plenty of things she would rather do, after all. There were people it was much more fun to play with or walk to school with. Josie didn't want anyone to make her better. So why should she try to force her to join in things, or to be good at anything?

"We told Miss Lawson you could sing. Why didn't you sing then?" Anita said fiercely, as soon as the bell had gone.

"Oh, leave her alone, 'Nita," said Jackie, dispiritedly. "She don't want to sing, like Miss Lawson said, she don't want to do nothing."

She turned away, then something woke up in Josie at last. "I do!" she burst out. "I want to sing."

The other two looked at each other.

"Why didn't you sing then, when you had the chance?"

Josie shuffled her feet.

"Dunno," she muttered.

"Would you sing now if she gave you another chance?" demanded Jackie.

"Yes," muttered Josie.

"If we could get Miss Lawson to come to hear you, you would sing to her?" said Anita.

"Yes," said Josie, still more definitely.

They looked at each other again.

"I'll go and ask," said Anita. "You stay here and practise it with her. You better sing, too," she threatened, going off towards the Staff Room.

"Come on," said Jackie, hope filling her again, "sing it through with me."

She began to sing, and Josie joined in. She sang loud and confidently.

"Cor! That was good," said Jackie, admiringly. "You sing it again by yourself, just so you can practise in the hall."

Up at the Staff Room door Anita was pleading with her teacher. Miss Lawson was getting ready to go home.

"Don't bother me," she said to Anita. "If Josie isn't prepared to sing in front of the class, it won't be any use giving her a part in the operetta. Besides, she won't be there on the night. She's just not reliable."

Miss Roberts was coming up the stairs, and Anita stood aside politely so that she could go into the Staff Room.

"What's this?" asked Miss Roberts, from inside the Staff Room. "Can *you* get Josie Pugsey to sing, Miss Lawson? I haven't heard a sound from her for the last two years."

"She *can* sing, Miss—honest!" implored Anita. "She got a lovely voice." (Anita really hadn't listened to Josie singing, but she was getting carried away.) "She says she wants to sing in the operetta, she just said so, to us. She'd sing to you now, Miss, if you came down to the hall."

Miss Lawson hesitated and looked at Miss Roberts.

"I'd give a lot to hear that child make any sort of noise," said Miss Roberts. "I'd like to come down with you, if you're going to hear her, may I?"

"Well, all right," said Miss Lawson, "but don't be surprised if she stands there, staring as if she's seen a ghost."

She shrugged, and led the way downstairs. Anita followed, and she found herself praying now.

"Oh, *please* make Josie sing!"

They heard the voice even before they got into the hall, a deep voice, clear and full.

It's the only life worth living,
So I'll live it, and I'll be it—the best for God.

Miss Lawson would not believe that it was Josie she had heard, and so insisted on her singing it through again, and this time Josie did. Jackie had to help her start, but then she sang it right through, and when she had finished the two teachers looked at each other, astonished, and Jackie and Anita looked at each other triumphantly.

"You certainly sing very nicely, Josie," said Miss Lawson, blinking at her as if she thought there might possibly be something wrong with her eyes, and she might not really be seeing Josie Pugsey at all. "We'll write a song for you in the operetta, if you would really like to sing it. Would you?"

"Yes," said Josie, "I'd like to sing in the operetta."

She was upright and confident. It was the first time Miss Lawson and Miss Roberts had seen her like that.

"I'd like you to be a peasant woman still," said Miss Lawson, "but we'll give you a song to sing on your own. We'll sort it out tomorrow."

Jackie, Anita and Josie went home singing. They went arm in arm and sang all the choruses they had ever learnt, all the way from the Blackwall Tunnel to the block where Anita and Josie lived. The loungers and the shoppers on the East India Dock Road stared at them and smiled good-temperedly. The traffic tried to drown their voices, but they only raised them the more. The wind blew dust in their throats, they had to stop and cough, but they began to sing again and nothing could stop them.

CHAPTER 7

Josie was in her hide-out again. She had not been there except on Saturdays and Sundays since that first week of term, the day she had first seen Lindy and envied Jackie the possession of a little sister. She had been coming to school so regularly that there hadn't been time for the hide-out, except at weekends.

After she had stolen the skipping rope, she had wanted to get away to the hide-out very badly indeed, but her dad had been at home all that week. When he'd heard about the skipping rope—they couldn't hide it because Mr. Humphreys had sent one of Josie's brothers home to fetch her mum, and he'd told the whole story—he had shouted and sworn at Josie, and hit her a lot. So much that she'd fallen and twisted her foot and couldn't walk properly for the next three days. But they had left her alone in the bedroom of the flat.

But Josie had nearly forgotten about those days now. She was happier than she had ever been in her life. Mrs. Smith had been letting her take Lindy down to the swings every day after school, and Lindy seemed to like her. She would be on Jackie's doorstep waiting for Josie, every day, and would come trotting down the street with squeals of joy as soon as she saw them come round the corner.

One day Josie had tried to take Lindy to the hide-out, but it had been too high. She couldn't heave her to the top of the wall, and Lindy couldn't climb.

Josie wondered if Jackie would be able to manage it. She would like to show someone her hide-out—one of her friends, of course. She wondered if Jackie would be able to manage the worst bit, where you had to wriggle off the roof and down on to the window frame. She had nearly fallen herself once when a tile had come loose in her hand, and Jackie hadn't got such long legs.

Anita was taller—but would probably refuse to spoil her clothes. No, if it was anyone, it would have to be Jackie. The hide-out would be a good place to practise for the operetta (which was to be held on November 4th, less than two weeks' time). Josie had been given a song for it, and Jackie had taught her how to read the words. She had learnt them now, and could sing them without her piece of paper, though she took it with her everywhere. She got it out now, and "read" the words aloud:

> My home was far across the sea,
> It's all that ever was home to me,
> But they burnt it down,
> And my field has gone,
> They were all that ever was home to me.

She knew the tune, too, and had sung it in front of the whole class last week. For the first time in her life, she had felt part of what was going on at school. The others had come round her and told her what a nice voice she had. And last week she had skipped a hundred skips without stopping. She went to and from school with Jackie and Anita and they skipped or sang all the time. They practised all the operetta words continually. Josie was happier than she had ever been in her whole life and she wanted to share her hide-out with Jackie. She sang her song aloud in the empty room, and noticed the way it echoed. She would like Jackie to hear that.

* * * * *

Jackie and Anita and Colin were coming home from Sunday School. Anita had been invited to tea at Jackie's house and they were going to watch "The Cavemen" on television. This was a serial which they liked very much, because it had prehistoric monsters and ferocious cavemen in it, all waging war against a family who had somehow got mixed up in time and gone backwards thousands of years. Their adventures and narrow escapes from death were recorded every Sunday at 4.30. Both Jackie and Anita privately imagined that when they were grown up they would somehow become like Corrinne, a girl who had a habit of being captured by cavemen or prehistoric animals each week, coming out of it unscathed in the nick of time. There was a good man called Jim who always did the right thing, and a silly one called Ferdinand who wore glasses and got himself and the others into trouble all the time. Jackie used to tease Colin by saying he was very like Ferdinand.

"What do you think'll happen?" said Anita. "That dinosaur's head was just coming up to the ledge—d'you think Corrinne'll find a way off the ledge?"

"She can't," said Jackie, positively, "there wasn't no opening in the wall of the cave—she've looked all round once."

"But she always gets out—what d'you think'll happen?"

"I 'spect Jim'll come up behind the dinosaur and shoot it just in time."

Colin gave a yelp, leapt a foot and a half into the air and gave an imitation of a dinosaur, shot at and dying.

"Looks like a dying duck to me," said Anita. "Hey! Look where you're going!"

Someone had come running round the corner, and Colin, doing a twist, had butted her in the stomach. They both fell down in a heap. The girls helped them up and dusted them down. The other one was Josie. She didn't cry, but Jackie noticed her knee.

"Here—your knee's bleeding. You better have it bandaged."

Suddenly she remembered the flat Josie lived in and Josie's mum and dad.

"Come home with me and my mum'll bandage it for you."

Josie's face lit up. On the way home she said, "Where you been?"

"Sunday School," said Anita. "Why don't you come too?"

"Oh, no!" said Josie, mysterious and important. "I got somewhere I goes on Sundays."

"Where d'you go?"

"Not telling you," said Josie, feeling more important still.

"D'you go to your gran's?"

"Haven't got no gran."

"Yes, you have," said Jackie quickly, "I seen your gran. She knows my mum, so there."

Caught out in a lie, Josie looked confused and mumbled something. Jackie felt cross. It was important to tell the truth—and to have friends who told the truth. She wished she hadn't asked Josie to come home and have her knee bandaged. She would probably always be a thief and tell lies. Anita said quickly, triumphantly, "Well, you been to your gran's then?"

"No, I ain't."

"Well, why don't you tell us where you been?" asked Jackie, angrily.

"I ain't going to tell you—it's a secret. I ain't been to my gran's, I never goes to my gran's."

"Liar!" said Anita.

"Come on!" said Jackie, in righteous indignation. "She tells lies."

They walked on to Jackie's house, which was only a few doors away, and Josie stood baffled and angry. In her loss and dismay she roared after them the worst swear word she knew, and then felt, as she saw Jackie's look of contempt, that she had lost their friendship for ever.

CHAPTER 8

Anita had had a tickle in her throat all day Sunday, and by Monday morning it had developed into a streaming cold. Irene, leaving for her job in the city, called in at Mrs. Smith's to tell her that Anita wouldn't be coming to school, and would Jackie please tell the teacher.

"You and Josie'll have to go on your own this morning," called Mrs. Smith, up the stairs. "Hurry up, Jackie, love."

She had heard about the quarrel but, in the way grown-ups have, had not taken it seriously.

"I ain't going with that Josie Pugsey," said Jackie, coming downstairs. "She's a liar—I ain't calling for her."

"Look, Jackie," said Mrs. Smith, "that's not the right way at all. Nobody's perfect. She only told one lie. Are you going to tell me you never told one?"

Jackie coloured. "Well, I never said I hadn't got a gran when I have."

"It don't make no difference," said Mrs. Smith. "A lie's a lie. It don't have to be the same one. Now don't try to tell me you ain't never told a lie."

"Well, I ain't calling for her anyway," muttered Jackie. "She can call for me for a change."

"I give up!" said Mrs. Smith helplessly. "You was all keen on helping Josie Pugsey the other day. You said you was going to do like the missionary did out there in Vietnam."

"Well, she don't get no better," said Jackie, crossly. "It ain't worth it."

"That's not true, neither," said Mrs. Smith. "I've seen a change in her, for one. You got to go on loving people when you're a Christian. 'T'aint no use starting off well and then giving up, so you remember that, if you calls yourself a Christian. Now go on or you'll be late—here's an apple."

Jackie walked down the street towards the block, wondering. She did call herself a Christian—she was sure she was—ever since last summer, but she had expected Josie not to do any bad things any more and she'd been disappointed in her. Anyway, why should she have to call for Josie? She could come downstairs, couldn't she? She knew what time Jackie got there. She decided to wait for a minute outside the block and see if Josie came down.

It was a frosty morning, although a pale gold sun was peering sleepily through the haze behind the block. Jackie was standing in the shadow and it was cold. She skipped to keep herself warm and counted —"hundred and fifty, hundred and fifty-one, hundred and fifty-two—ouch!" She felt her rope trodden on from behind and turned to see Mark grinning. He had stepped on it very expertly.

"You mean thing! What do you think you're doing?"

"Well, you'll never make it to school like that," said Mark. "You're just skipping on the spot, you ain't moving at all."

"I'm waiting for Josie Pugsey—least, I'm waiting to see if she comes down."

"Seen this?" Mark put his hand over a lump in his

coat pocket and brought it out. "It's a bat. I'm taking it to show Miss Lawson."

"Cor!" Jackie peered at the black furry thing. "Where'd you get that?"

"Found it yesterday. We went down my uncle's. He knows a man who got a farm. Here, I'll tell you about it if you're coming. But I'm not waiting here for Josie Pugsey. She ain't coming today, I shouldn't think."

Jackie gave in without a fight. She was bored with waiting for Josie on her own, and she wanted to ask Mark all about the farm and everything he'd done. Besides, Josie never had anything interesting to talk about when they went to school. She'd never done anything interesting even when they could make her talk about it. She didn't watch television, she said, though they had it in their flat. What did she do when she was at home then, Jackie had asked once?

"Nothing."

"Well, you must be doing something."

"I just sits down."

"Well, what do you do when you're sitting down?"

"Nothing."

Mark, on the other hand, had been to a farm in Essex, and had seen all the tractors and farming machines, and had climbed around in barns and hay lofts, and had made a house in the hay with his two cousins. It was in the hay loft they'd found the bat, hanging upside down.

"What you going to do with it?"

"I thought we could keep it in school along with the other pets, the hamsters and guinea-pigs."

"Can you keep it in a cage? I don't think you keep bats in cages, do you?"

"We'll have to have a perch, I 'spect," said Mark, cheerfully.

In no time at all they were at school and the others were crowding round to see the bat.

Josie had waited for Anita to call, and then had remembered the quarrel, and in her confusion had not known what to do. She had waited till she was almost late, and then had slipped out of the flat, banging the door on the twins who were crawling about after her. Both her mum and her dad were in bed, and the two older boys had gone on to school, or somewhere else, perhaps. There was no sign of Anita on the stairs and no sign of Jackie outside. There was, however, Larry O'Dare, letting out a nasty-sounding "Ho! Ho!" as he came down the stairs behind her.

Josie glanced nervously back over her shoulder. She had a bit of a start, but she knew she had to pass Larry O'Dare's Comprehensive School to get to St. Barnabas. That meant he would be coming behind her all the way, and his mates joining him most likely. Josie's knee was stiff, and she could not run properly. She hurried, limping, across the playground, and heard the voice behind.

"Ho! Ho! I'll get you, Pugsey brat—no hurry, plenty of time."

Josie turned quickly down a side street and then up another. She heard a whistle and a shout and began to try and run. It sounded as if one of Larry's mates had joined him and they were laughing and coming after her. She turned up a lane and saw a garage with double doors and a lorry parked inside. There was no one there and she slipped in and hid behind one of the doors. It was only just in time, for the boys were running up the lane.

"Where's she gone?" she heard one of them say.

They went on up the lane and into the next street. Josie relaxed, but at that moment a man came into the garage. He went to the other side of the lorry and Josie slipped outside into the lane. Her heart was thumping and she didn't know which way to go in case she bumped into Larry O'Dare and his mates.

She went back down the lane the way she had come, approaching the corner cautiously, her legs shaking. No, they were not in that street. But they would have to be in school soon, and she dared not go towards St. Barnabas, past the Comprehensive.

She turned and took the opposite direction and found her feet taking her along the back streets and the lanes towards the wharves. Towards the only place in the world where she felt safe—towards her hide-out.

* * * * *

Miss Lawson was having a practice for the operetta at 2.30.

"We've less than a fortnight," she said, "so I hope you all know your parts and the words of the songs. We'll have a quick run through, and then I'll tell you about the costumes you'll need."

It went pretty well, but with a few snags, of course. There was some chattering on the part of the peasants and Miss Lawson made them stop their song and start all over again. Then the soldiers came on.

"We don't seem to have many soldiers, where are they all?" wondered Miss Lawson, looking puzzled.

"Oh, Miss!" squeaked Sharon, remembering. "It's Mark and Billy, Miss."

"They're outside Mr. Humphreys' room, Miss," said Les.

"Why? What have they done?"

"Mr. Humphreys found them climbing on a window, Miss," Paul joined in with the story.

"Yes, Miss, they said they was measuring it, Miss."

Miss Lawson turned away from them, but the class saw the smile she was squashing down.

"Oh, well, we'll do without them for now, I suppose. Let's try the first soldiers' song all together."

After the first soldiers' song came the second peasants' song, and the verse that Josie was to sing on her own. It was only now that Miss Lawson looked round and remembered that Josie was absent.

"Josie Pugsey's absent, so we'll do it without her bit."

Jackie had a bit of a shock when she said that, and felt as guilty as if she herself were Josie Pugsey. She had completely forgotten about Josie, and Anita too, for that matter. She wondered if there was anything the matter with Josie, or if she was just staying away for nothing. Perhaps she had better call for her tomorrow and see.

Accordingly, the next day Jackie traipsed right up three flights of stone steps to be greeted by Mrs. Pugsey in a dirty dressing-gown with a cigarette stuck to her lower lip, as usual.

"Aw, she've gone on," and she slammed the door.

Gone on? Why? Jackie had left earlier than usual. She did not know that Josie had left still earlier, so as to avoid Larry O'Dare, and having successfully managed this, she was skipping in the frosty playground, waiting for Jackie to come and join her. She skipped awkwardly; her hurt knee had a large and dirty rag tied round it, and she held that leg out in front and hopped on the other one. But she was so much better at skipping that she managed to go right round the playground without stopping.

Jackie arrived, having come alone as Anita was still in bed with the cold. When she saw Josie's back view hopping stiffly away from her around the playground, her fury rose up inside her. Didn't she always go and call for Josie? And hadn't she been the one to get her a part in the operetta? Hadn't she helped her with skipping and given her the rope? And she'd helped her learn the operetta songs. And Josie had gone on. That was all the thanks she got when she called. Well, she wouldn't call again, Josie Pugsey could look after herself now. She turned her back and went to play with Sharon and Marissa, and she didn't speak to Josie all day.

The next day Josie was absent from school, and she did not turn up on Thursday or Friday either. On Friday afternoon there was an operetta practice, and Miss Lawson called Jackie up and told her to tell Anita about the actions they were to do with the songs and the kind of dress Anita needed to bring.

"Will she be back on Monday?" she asked.

"I think so, Miss, she only got a cold."

"Well, that's all right then—oh, by the way, do you know anything about Josie Pugsey? Don't you come to school with her?"

"Yes, Miss, I used to," said Jackie, defensively. "We used to call for her, Miss, but last time her mum said she'd gone on, so I don't call any more."

"Do you know if she's ill?"

"No, Miss, I dunno."

"Well, if she doesn't come on Monday she won't be able to have a part," said Miss Lawson, looking hard at Jackie. "Will you tell her that if you see her?"

Jackie felt most uncomfortable. She decided to call at Auntie Marge's and see if Anita was better, then maybe she'd see Josie out playing somewhere, and she could give her Miss Lawson's message with a clear conscience. Maybe she would even offer to call for her again. But there was nobody in the playground except a few younger boys and girls whom Jackie did not know, and there was nobody on the stairs all the way up to the fifth floor either. Auntie Marge opened the door of the flat.

"Aw, *you* again, what d'you want?" she said, teasing Jackie, who stood her ground firmly.

"I come to see Anita, of course. Is she better?"

"Well, I s'pose I better let you in then, if you've come to see "Er 'Ighness'. For a minute, I thought you might've come to see your old auntie."

"Oh, I have, too," said Jackie obediently, and she reached up to kiss Auntie Marge. "But I've got an important message from school for Anita, I'd better tell you too, I think," she added. "It's about Anita's costume for the operetta."

Anita was up and looked pleased to see Jackie. Apart from a rather red nose, there did not seem to be anything wrong with her. Jackie explained her business, and Auntie Marge said she would see what dresses she could find for them both. Auntie Marge had a huge old suitcase under the bed in her room which had some very exciting things in it—old gold and silver shoes, her wedding dress, a very grand affair in white satin and organza frills, and some Indian things which Uncle Sid had brought back from the war. The girls loved going through this suitcase, and looked hopeful when Auntie Marge said she would look out some dressing-up things.

"I ain't going to do nothing now, so it's no good you lookin' at me like that," she said, however. "Them boys'll be in and I gotta go down the shop and get some pie and mash. I ain't had no time for cooking, looking after 'Madam' here." She nodded at Anita. "We'll have a look after tea. Now behave yourselves." And she went.

Anita and Jackie spent the next ten minutes practising the actions to go with the songs in the operetta. The telly was making a noise, so they went into Anita's bedroom to practise. It was Irene's bedroom as well, so after they'd got tired of practising, they peeped at Irene's dresses in the wardrobe and tried on some of her high-heeled shoes and her lipstick and eye pencils. Then they laughed at each other.

"You don't half look funny," giggled Anita. "You got black stuff all down one side of your nose."

"Well, you got two black eyes then," said Jackie. "You look just like someone hit you."

They both roared with laughter and began to dance around the room, ending up doing acrobats on the bed. Then they heard Auntie Marge coming in.

"Quick, we better get this stuff off!"

They began dabbing madly with lumps of cottonwool. Anita copied what she thought Irene did, and Jackie copied what Anita was doing, but the cottonwool wouldn't seem to get the stuff off—instead it smudged and looked ten times worse. At the moment when they looked woefully at each other and admitted defeat, the bedroom door opened.

"I thought you was quiet!" Auntie Marge looked very grim. The cousins stared at her full of guilt. Suddenly she roared with loud laughter.

"What a pair! I never seen anything so funny! I wish I had a camera."

The two giggled self-consciously, then they all laughed again together.

After that Auntie Marge said to Jackie, "Well, you better stay to tea. I can't send you home like that, can I?"

Jackie was delighted, they'd have pie and mash, and then she and Anita could spend the evening playing and watching telly. She'd missed Anita all the week, but hadn't realized it till now.

"How'll we tell mum? She'll be expecting me," she

said anxiously, afraid Auntie Marge would send her out in the street with her highly-coloured face, and everyone she met would stare and laugh.

"Ow! I seen that girl Josie Pugsey playing on the landing. I'll ask her to run a message for me," said Auntie Marge. "I'll give her five pence for going, she don't get nothing much, poor kid."

While Auntie Marge had popped out to find Josie, Jackie remembered about Miss Lawson's warning and told Anita.

"Well, ain't she been to school this week then?" asked Anita, bewildered. Jackie explained how she'd waited for a bit on Monday and then gone on with Mark, and how Josie hadn't come. And then she'd gone to call on Tuesday and Josie had gone on without her, so she'd got fed up and hadn't called again and Josie hadn't been to school the rest of the week.

"Miss Lawson asked me if I knew what was the matter with her," she ended. "Do you know, 'Nita?"

"Well, I saw her," said Anita. "I saw her today. I went out this morning with mum—first time this week—and I saw Josie going down the stairs, and I said, 'Going to school, Josie?' and she nodded her head."

"So she was telling another lie then," said Jackie severely. "She ain't no good, is she?"

The door bell of the flat rang just then, and Anita went to answer it, thinking it was Frankie. But instead Josie Pugsey stood outside the door. She stared, entranced, at Anita's smudged and coloured eyes.

"What do you want, Josie Pugsey?" asked Anita, in a rude voice.

"I got a message for Jackie," said Josie, deeply, but she flinched at Anita's voice.

"Jackie got a message for you too," said Anita. "From Miss Lawson. Tell her, Jackie."

"Let her tell me my message first," said Jackie.

"It's a secret," said Josie. "I'm only tellin' *you*."

"Is it a message from my mum?"

"No. It's a secret I got to tell you."

"Well, you can tell Anita too, can't you?"

"No. I ain't gonna tell her."

"Did my mum say I gotta be back any special time?"

"No."

"Well, what is it then?"

"Ain't telling *her*." Josie looked sullenly at Anita.

"Well, it ain't no use telling *me* then, 'cos I don't want to hear it," said Jackie, her crossness getting the better of her. "Look, did you give that message to my mum?"

"Yes, I did." Josie grinned suddenly and showed them Auntie Marge's sixpence, "and I'm gonna buy some sweets and take them—somewhere—and you can come, if you like," she added, looking at Jackie.

"I don't want to come, thank you," said Jackie, thinking Auntie Marge's flat was the only place she wanted to be at present. "But you better come to school on Monday or Miss Lawson says you can't have a part in the operetta."

Josie looked struck. Her mouth dropped open; she looked as if she had suddenly remembered the operetta.

"Yeah!" Anita joined in. "You better come to school, we only got till Friday, then we're doing it."

Josie took a step backwards.

"*You* ain't been to school," she stated accusingly. Anita was filled with righteous indignation.

"I been ill!" she shouted. "*You* ain't been ill."

Josie backed away and began to retreat down the stairs. "I don't care," she said suddenly, very loudly.

"No, you don't care about nothing," shouted Anita, coming after her to the head of the stairs. She let her temper run right away with her this time, and began to shout horribly at Josie, who started going down the stairs, away from Anita, as quickly as she could.

"You let Miss Lawson down, and you let our team down—you're no good. You just stays away from school for nothing! You ain't ill! You just plays around! Jackie said you weren't in school today and you told me you was going to school! You're a liar! You'll have the attendance man round to see your dad, you will."

Josie had retreated practically all the way back down to her own landing, and Anita shouted down the well of the stairs, her voice echoing back from the bare brick walls. Jackie did not join in and felt a bit uncomfortable. She stood back in the doorway of the flat, and suddenly she heard a man's rough voice saying something she didn't catch. It came suddenly up from a landing down below, and it sounded fierce and threatening. At the same time there was a yelp of terror, and Anita suddenly stopped shouting and leaned over the banister to see. The voice began again and continued in a roar. There were more yelps and squeals, and then the sound of blows and scuffling and screams. The screams were in Josie's voice. Jackie rushed to the banister but she couldn't see anything. The voices got further away and were cut off as a door slammed. Jackie looked at Anita. She had gone white under the eye make-up and lipstick.

"It was her dad," she whispered. "He got hold of

her. He was waiting at the bottom of the stairs, and she was looking back up here, and he caught hold of her and he had his belt in one hand. I think he heard what I said. I think he's hitting her awful hard."

*   *   *   *   *

It was late that night when the door of the Pugseys' flat opened carefully and slowly, and a little figure crept out. It had a thick coat, which was too big for it, and a pair of plimsolls, which were about the right size. It shut the door of the flat carefully, and, looking sharply all around, descended the stone stairs. It was limping and could not seem to move as swiftly as it would like. At the bottom of the stairs it paused, then limped across the empty moonlit playground and hurried into the cover of the shadowy back streets. Along street after street it went, pulling back into doorways at the slightest sound, ducking down behind a wall if a car passed by, until it reached an empty street with great gates across it, rattling eerily in the night wind.

The moon shone high, bright, cold on the little shadow climbing the wall, pulling, scraping and slipping. It had to make several attempts before its hands grasped the top, but it was up there at last. Then it crawled up the roof, swung itself over the edge and disappeared.

CHAPTER 9

Jackie was not in the mood for Lindy's playing about. The usual Saturday morning palaver of washing and dressing her small sister was irksome to her. Besides, it was cold up in the bathroom. She wanted to get down to the living room by the stove, but Lindy wouldn't take her pyjamas off. She rolled herself up in the blankets on Jackie's bed and refused to budge. Jackie's fingers got colder and colder. In the end, she said she was leaving Lindy up there all day and, if she didn't behave herself, she didn't care, she would go down by the fire and read a book. She really had no patience this morning, she thought to herself. She was so cross she smacked Lindy, and made her cry. Then, of course, Mrs. Smith came upstairs, exasperated, and told Jackie to go on down and she would dress Lindy herself.

"It isn't much I ask you to do on a Saturday," she added, "but you don't try to help. You know I've got a lot to do, but you can't even look after your little sister in peace. Some girls would give their eyes to have a lovely little sister like you got."

Jackie went downstairs and huddled by the stove with her book. But she couldn't get into it, it was such a cold day. Winter had come all of a sudden, and there was a great wind tearing down the tiny back-yards between the houses—a wind that was almost a gale. She couldn't go out to play in that. Auntie Marge wouldn't let Anita out in it, she knew. Saturday stretched before her, empty and boring—there was nothing to do at all.

Colin was playing with his garage and cars all over the living room. He was making all the right noises and, of course, making a great deal of them. Jackie couldn't concentrate on her book at all. Then Mrs. Smith brought Lindy down and the noise was doubled. Lindy pushed herself back and forth in her little wooden truck, singing loudly. Jackie was fed up with her family.

"Mum, where can I go?" she asked complainingly at the scullery door.

"You'll have to go to the shops for me," said Mrs. Smith firmly. "Now don't pull that face, you haven't done nothing else all morning. You can go down the market as soon as I've made a list out."

Jackie struggled down the road against the wind, which was trying to tear her shopping bag off her arm. She thought that, since she was outside, she might as well call and see Anita on the way back, and maybe Auntie Marge would ask her to tea again. The pie and mash had been lovely last night. They had put a nice lot of vinegar all over the mash, and the pie had had beautifully flaky pastry. But she hadn't enjoyed the taste quite as much as she'd expected. Was it that Josie Pugsey had spoilt everything? Oh, why did she care if Josie Pugsey's dad hit her? She'd deserved it, hadn't she? She'd stayed away from school without telling anyone and without being ill. Did she get hit like that every time her dad found out about her staying away from school? She must've been hit an awful lot, so why didn't she stop doing it then?

She was so stupid though—Josie Pugsey was the stupidest girl she knew. Jackie was glad she wasn't Josie. For a moment she even appreciated Lindy and Colin and their noise. She was glad her dad was quiet and kind and played games with them when he got home from work. She couldn't ever remember her dad hitting her.

She did the shopping—counting the change rather abstractedly, and not being sure if she'd got it right (Mrs. Smith was rather fussy about the change being right). Then Jackie made her way back along the street which would lead to Anita's block. Walking along, the wind behind her this time, she passed the Bible Shop. She stopped to look at the pictures in the window, and there, inside the shop, she saw Miss Roberts, who was buying some pictures. They must be the prizes which were given for thirty attendances at the Bible Club. Jackie knew she was due for one at half-term, so she paused, leaning against the wind and waiting for Miss Roberts to come out of the shop. A piece of paper blew up and tried to wrap itself round her leg, and as she bent to knock it away Miss Roberts came out and nearly fell over her. She dropped a little package she was carrying, and the wind took it and whisked it along the pavement. Jackie retrieved it, in spite of her shopping, and brought it back.

"Here you are, Miss."

"Oh, hullo, Jackie. Sorry for falling over you. What were you doing?"

Jackie explained about the paper and hung about eyeing the packages. "Are them the prizes for the Bible Club, Miss?" she asked.

"Well, some of them," Miss Roberts replied, "and

some of them are book-markers to give to my Sunday class. Do you think they'll like them?"

She brought out a coloured book-marker. It was in red and white with a picture of a boy helping another one up who had fallen down and was crying. There was a verse underneath.

"Coo! Ain't that good?" exclaimed Jackie, in admiration. "Ain't that good, Miss?"

She wished she was in Miss Roberts' Sunday class.

Miss Roberts said suddenly, "You can have that one, Jackie, if you like—I bought one too many."

"Can I? Oh, thank you, Miss."

She clutched the book-marker tightly and set off to show it to Anita. What a good thing she'd come out shopping for her mum just then, and had met Miss Roberts! The day was not so bad after all. In a sheltered corner, she stopped and looked at her prize again, and this time she read the verse.

"He is kind unto the unthankful," she read slowly aloud. "Be ye therefore merciful."

She put the marker into the pocket of her mac, and went on along the street, memorizing the verse without realizing she was doing it.

"He is kind unto the unthankful." That meant God was kind to people who didn't say "thank you".

"Be ye therefore merciful." That meant Christians had to be kind to people as well, even if they didn't say "thank you". She felt pleased with herself for knowing what it meant. She would tell Miss Roberts on Monday, but she knew it was right.

She began climbing the stairs of Anita's block, and saw Mrs. Pugsey coming towards her. Mrs. Pugsey didn't look clean or tidy, but she didn't have a cigarette in her mouth. She stopped in front of Jackie, blocking her way, and her eyes stared and she was biting her lips.

"You ain't seen my Josie, have you?" she asked, very short and abrupt.

"No, I ain't seen her," said Jackie, startled. "Where's she gone?"

"I dunno," said Mrs. Pugsey, looking past Jackie into the playground. "She wasn't there this morning. I ain't seen her since last night."

"Do you think she got up early and went out without telling you?" asked Jackie, alarmed.

"I dunno—I suppose so," said Mrs. Pugsey, helplessly. "I ain't seen her since last night. I thought she'd gone to bed. Tell her to come home if you see her."

"Yes, all right," said Jackie. She went on upstairs, and Mrs. Pugsey went on out of the block.

When Anita heard, she said at once, "Do you think she've run away, Jackie?"

Jackie hadn't thought of it, but Mrs. Pugsey had certainly seemed worried.

"I think I'll tell mum," said Jackie. "She'll know what to do."

She took the shopping home and reported the news to Mrs. Smith. Her mother looked at the kitchen clock.

"Good gracious!" she said. "It's twelve o'clock now, and Mrs. Pugsey ain't seen Josie since last night! She ought've told the police."

"Maybe she only went out this morning," said Jackie. "Her mum don't always get up in the mornings. Josie often gets up and comes to school and her mum's still in bed. I asked her sometimes when we used to call for her."

"Well!" said Mrs. Smith. "I suppose it's no business of ours."

But all the same, at about three o'clock that afternoon, she suddenly called Jackie away from her cosy armchair by the telly.

"Tell you what," she said, "you go round and see if Josie's come back home yet."

"Aw, mum," protested Jackie, "I don't like going round there."

"You go round there," said Mrs. Smith, "and then we'll have fish and chips tonight, for a treat."

"Promise?"

"Promise. Off you go."

It was horrible, turning out into the cold again.

"It's nearly November," thought Jackie. "Soon it'll be firework night, and 'Nita's birthday."

Anita always had a party on her birthday. It was the best party of the year, Jackie thought. They went over to their gran's at Dagenham and built a bonfire in her back garden. Torches and rockets and squibs—and burnt sausages—yum!

She climbed up the three flights to the Pugseys' flat. She was getting sick of traipsing up and down these stairs. She dreaded knocking on the door, and was in two minds as to whether she should fetch Anita down first to keep her company. Then she put her left hand in her pocket, and felt the book-marker Miss Roberts had given her. She pulled it out and read the verse again—"He is kind to the unthankful . . . Be ye therefore merciful". Jackie remembered the first time she had ever knocked on the Pugseys' door, and how ungrateful Mrs. Pugsey had been when they'd returned the slipper. Then, with deepening shame, she remembered their anger and her own resentment at Josie recently. She had felt that Josie Pugsey hadn't been grateful enough for all she had done. She'd been fed up with Josie.

"Be ye therefore merciful."

Jackie remembered Josie's standing with a bleeding knee and that bewildered look on her face—and herself shouting "You're a liar!" And then she remembered something that had been nagging at her off and on since that Sunday afternoon—that she herself had declared she had seen Josie's gran, when really she had never set eyes on her. So she, as well as Josie, had been telling a lie. She remembered Josie saying she had a secret to share with her, and she had answered that she didn't want to know. She was so ashamed and so busy thinking of all this that she stood in front of the Pugseys' door for some time, holding her bookmarker, without knocking.

"Oh, God, I'm sorry," she whispered, at last. "I haven't done what that missionary did. I didn't keep it up. I'm sorry, God." She felt relieved once she'd said this, and so she knocked on the door.

It was opened by the terrible Mr. Pugsey. Jackie was very much put off, because she hadn't expected him to be there.

"Please, please, can I see—Josie?" she stuttered.

He glowered at her horribly.

"Ain't here!" he growled.

"Oh." Jackie turned, only too thankful to get away.

"Wait a minute," he roared, "come 'ere."

Jackie shook from head to foot, and wished someone would come up the stairs. She turned back very slowly.

"If you sees her, tell her to come on home, her mum's out looking for 'er," said Mr. Pugsey. Then he went into the flat again and slammed the door. Jackie went down three flights of stairs faster than she'd ever moved before, and at the bottom stood still with her legs feeling like two pillars of jelly. She thought for the first time—and with a sense of shock—that Josie Pugsey must have spent most of her life feeling just like this. She went slowly out into the playground, looking down, thinking. . . . Whiz! Something shot past her ear and landed with a clatter on the ground behind her. Surprised, Jackie looked behind.

The great rough lout called Larry O'Dare was sitting on the wall at the other side of the playground. Even as she looked at him in astonishment, he picked up another stone and threw it. Jackie fled in horror, her heart thudding in her ears. She was so upset that she burst into tears the moment she got safely on to her own doorstep. Her dad opened the door, and she fell in, sobbing. Mr. Smith picked her up, saw there were no cuts or bruises, carried her into the living room and sat down with Jackie on his knee, and his nice, strong arms around her.

"It was that Larry O'Dare," sobbed Jackie. "I didn't do nothing and he threw stones."

"Did they hit you?"

"No-o."

"Well, I think in that case," said Mr. Smith, considering, "a nice bit of chocolate might help."

He pulled a bar out of his pocket, and divided it into five, giving Jackie the biggest share.

After this Mr. Smith heard all about the Pugseys, and how Mrs. Pugsey was out looking for Josie.

"I know where she is," said Lindy, brightly, sitting up among her building bricks on the floor. Mrs. Smith laughed and jerked a thumb in Lindy's direction.

"Hark at her! You'd think she knew all about it!"

Jackie had a sudden idea.

"I know! S'pose Josie's run away and is hiding. I bet she'd come out if she saw Lindy. She likes Lindy, don't she?"

Mrs. Smith considered this.

"Well, I think we ought to get the police if the child's missing."

"That's the Pugseys' job," said Mr. Smith. "You can't go and get the police unless Mrs. Pugsey asks you to, at least."

"Well, I tell you what," said Mrs. Smith, "I'll go out with Jackie and Lindy for a little while, and walk round and see if we can see Josie. Like Jackie says, if she's hiding, she might come out if she sees Lindy. And then, on the way home, we'll get us all some fish and chips for supper."

Jackie didn't feel like wrapping herself up and trudging out into the cold wind yet again, but she felt she should do it, without grumbling. She wanted to put right her failure to be a real friend to Josie, and felt that this was one of the ways.

Mrs. Smith got her shopping bag, and they walked along, each holding a hand of Lindy's, past the market and the pie and mash shop, up on to the East India Dock Road, down the subway and across the road to where the Blackwall Tunnel began. Lindy alternately skipped and hopped or dragged behind complaining about the wind. On the East India Dock Road the wind was tremendous; it seemed to be charging down the road faster than the great clattering lorries, and it still had time to pause and puff clouds of dust and grit in the direction of the walkers. Jackie's eyes felt as if they were full of stones, and her nose began to itch.

They went back under the subway and up the steps again to be met by a sudden gale that nearly blew them all into the road. They staggered across to the shelter of a wall and a great block of flats, dragging Lindy with them. The wind suddenly dropped, and they nearly fell over again because they had been leaning into it.

Mrs. Smith suddenly had a feeling that she ought to cross the road and go along in the direction of the wharves and warehouses. There were a number of condemned and derelict houses along the side streets in that direction, and she suspected that Josie might be hiding there.

"Oh, mum," said Jackie, weakening already, "do we have to? It's so cold, and the wind's nearly blowing us over."

"Just a bit more, Jackie, don't give up just yet. Come on, we'll cross at the lights."

They went out from the shelter of their wall into the full wind force again and crossed the road at the lights in a somewhat zig-zag manner. Then up a desolate side street, full of empty houses with old doors barricading all the shattered windows. The wind was against them now, and Jackie's eyes, which had just begun to clear, got filled up with grit and dust again. They put their heads down, half-closed their eyes and hurried along the sad little street. They seemed to wander up and down such streets for hours. Every so often they would huddle into one of the grimy doorways and Mrs. Smith would shout, "Josie! Josie Pugsey! Are you there?" through the letter-box. But the wind carried her words away half the time, and either it whisked the reply away, too, or there was nobody there to answer.

"Where we goin', Mum?" Lindy kept asking.

"Just a little walk, lovey, to see if we can find Josie."

Then they came into the street where Josie's warehouse was. It was empty, and just for a minute the wind dropped and Lindy exclaimed loudly, "I been here! I been here with Josie."

"Where? Where?" They both bent down anxiously.

"Here," said Lindy. "We——" and the wind, tearing at their coats and hair, charged up the street and nearly knocked them all over. It also blew Lindy's words away.

"We'll shelter by the wall," said Mrs. Smith, and they went over and leant against the wall Josie used to climb to reach her hide-out. It wasn't real shelter, but it was the only thing that street had to provide. Lindy was saying something, but the wind rattling the great doors to the wharf entrance was drowning her voice. Mrs. Smith and Jackie both stooped down again.

"Where did you go from here, Lindy?" said Mrs. Smith.

"Dunno," said Lindy.

They sighed and looked hopelessly at each other.

"She wanted to lift me over the wall," said Lindy, suddenly, in a calm period.

"What?"

"Up there," the child pointed up the high brick

wall. "She tried to climb the wall, and we both fell down and I scratched my arm and I cried."

"Oh, I remember, that time I let her take you for a walk and you came back all dirty!" Mrs. Smith looked horrified. "The naughty girl, what on earth was she doing?"

"What did you do then?" asked Jackie, desperately. "Quick! Where did you go next!"

Lindy looked blank.

"Dunno."

"Oh, come on! You *got* to know!"

Jackie almost stamped with impatience.

"Dunno," said Lindy, wide-eyed.

"Oh, mum, make her tell!"

"I can't, Jackie, don't go on at her. She can't remember things like you."

Mrs. Smith asked Lindy some persuading questions, but no answers were forthcoming. Lindy wanted to go home, and finally began to cry.

Cold, tired and fed up, they went back, through more desolate little streets, past more warehouses, back to the Blackwall Tunnel Road, with the wind jumping out on them from behind every corner. They got right back to the market, and Lindy was growing more cheerful at every step. She began to dance and wriggle and jump, and as they were nearly home again Mrs. Smith let go of her hand, so did Jackie. Lindy ran ahead and sheltered from the wind in a corner by the Post Office wall, waiting for them to come up. Mrs. Smith and Jackie walked along dispiritedly. Then Jackie began to cheer up as she remembered that mum had promised fish and chips for tea, and that they were nearly home. They had done their best to find Josie, but they couldn't, and that was that.

"Come on, Lindy," called Mrs. Smith, as they passed the corner, "nearly there now."

They went on a bit, then looked back, but Lindy was still in her corner, twinkling mischievously.

"Come on! Oh, do go and get her, Jackie," sighed Mrs. Smith. "I'll go on and get the fish and chips."

"Oh, mum!"

Jackie stalked balefully towards Lindy, who became wildly excited and jumped up and down, shouting, "Can't get me! Can't get me! I'm in my 'ide-out. You can't come in."

"Oh, come on—I've had enough nonsense!" Jackie was too tired to persuade with promises of a nice tea and some television. She grabbed her little sister and began to drag Lindy along. Lindy let out a yell that Mrs. Smith heard in spite of the wind. She turned back, really cross this time.

"It's my 'ide-out! Like Josie has! You can't get me! None of you can get me out of my 'ide-out."

Mrs. Smith said, "What's the matter *now*?"

"She keeps sayin' it's her 'ide-out' or something," said Jackie. "I don't know what she's talking about, but she said something about Josie."

"What is it, lovey?"

Lindy was silent.

"What's a 'ide-out? Oh, *I* know," Mrs. Smith turned to Jackie, light dawning, "she means a hiding-place."

She turned back to Lindy, teasing, playing the game for all she was worth.

"Where's your hide-out then, lovey? You show mum."

Lindy pointed to her corner.

"And where's *Josie's* hide-out?"

"Over the wall," said Lindy, confidently. "Over the big high wall."

"Was it the wall she tried to lift you over?"

"Yes," said Lindy, nodding hard, "and I was too heavy."

"*That* wall?" said Jackie, looking at her mother in despair. Mrs. Smith nodded.

Jackie groaned, "All that way back again? And we just come from there!"

CHAPTER 10

The evening dragged on and on. Jackie, waiting for her mother to come back, tried to read her book, and for the second time that day she failed. She fidgeted and thought uneasily of the wharves and Josie. She thought of the talk they'd had in school only last term, when a River Policeman had come to school and shown them a film and warned them of the dangers of the wharves. He had told them about the tides in the river and the danger of going near it, or of going near the mud at the riverside. And Josie had a hide-out somewhere over that high wall, maybe on a boat on the river. Perhaps this was the hide-out she'd been going to show Jackie—only Jackie hadn't been interested.

She wished her mother would come back. That afternoon they had trudged all the way back to the wall, battling with the wind, and having to take it in turns to carry a complaining Lindy. Then they had shouted and shouted "Josie! Josie!" till, what with the wind and the dust, they had no breath and no voices left. And the wall and the gate and the warehouse had given no reply. Only the gate had banged and banged against its bolts and padlocks, but they were quite sure it was the wind doing that, not Josie. In the end Jackie had taken Lindy on home, and Mrs. Smith had gone to see Mrs. Pugsey.

When Mrs. Smith had heard that Josie was still

missing, and that Mrs. Pugsey had searched everywhere, she told her what Lindy had said about the hide-out beyond the wall. Then she had gone to the police station with Mrs. Pugsey. She had called in briefly to say that this was what she was doing, and would Jackie put Lindy to bed and make Colin go when it was time. She would be back as soon as she could.

Jackie felt very depressed. Mr. Smith, to cheer them all up, went to the fish and chip shop and bought them all the promised supper, which had been forgotten till now. He even bought Jackie a big gherkin and an onion to go with it, and they all sat round the kitchen table and tried to enjoy themselves. But it didn't taste so nice, although Jackie put lashings of vinegar over it. Then Jackie and her dad put Lindy to bed, and just as Jackie was picking up Lindy's scattered clothes off the bedroom floor, she heard her mother's key turn in the lock of the front door.

She stood frozen for a minute, then raced to the top of the stairs.

"Mum! Mum! Have they found her? Is she all right?"

Mrs. Smith came into the hall, and she had an elderly woman behind her.

"Yes, Jackie love, it's all right. Josie's been found. This is Josie's gran. Now we want a little talk and a cup of tea, so you run along and watch telly."

Jackie couldn't concentrate on the telly. She was itching with impatience. Where had Josie been found? Had she run away to her gran's? Why had her gran come here? What was going to happen to Josie?

The minute Josie's gran left the house, Jackie rushed

upon her mother, and asked all the questions she could think of as fast as she could. Mrs. Smith took a deep breath, and began the answers.

"Mrs. Horton is Josie's gran, and she is going to offer to have Josie to live with her for the time being. At the moment Josie's in hospital. No, they don't think she's badly hurt, but she had a fall—seemed to have fallen out of the window of one of the warehouses and bumped her head. If it hadn't been for our Lindy pointing out that wall, they wouldn't have found her for much longer, because she'd fallen into a little yard that wasn't used at all."

"Oh!" Jackie heaved a sigh of relief. "Well, is she going to be in school on Monday?"

"Goodness me!" Mrs. Smith laughed. "I shouldn't think so. She knocked herself right out, you see. Lay there in the cold for hours and hours. I expect they'll keep her there till they're sure she's better, and feed her up a bit while they're deciding whether she's to go to her gran's."

"But the operetta—she'll miss her part!" Jackie was upset all over again. Mrs. Smith said, "Well, we'll see about it, I'm going to the hospital to see her tomorrow, and I'll see what the matron says."

* * * * *

It was Friday night, the night of the operetta. Class One had arrived and were putting on their costumes in the classroom. Jackie had a mustard-coloured tablecloth draped over one shoulder and under the other. Anita had a green shawl and a brown skirt which came down to her ankles. Miss Lawson was applying brown greasepaint to everyone, a broad stripe across the forehead, one down the nose and each side of the cheek, then across the chin. Then they had to rub it in. Everybody was running around, showing their costumes to everybody else. Janet was having great difficulty pinning on her nurse's cap, and Jackie offered to do it for her. She was engrossed in this when she heard Anita's voice.

"Look, Jackie! Look at the door."

"Just a minute—I'm doing up this pin. . . ."

Jackie glanced up and then stayed, staring.

"Ow!" said Janet, "hurry up! You're digging it in!"

"Oh, look!" said Jackie. "It's Josie, look!"

Josie had come shyly into the classroom with a strange lady behind her. The strange lady began talking to Miss Lawson, and Miss Lawson smiled down at Josie as she listened.

Josie looked quite different. She was clean—Jackie had never seen her so clean. Her hair was cut short, just like a boy's, and it had gone a lot fairer. In fact, it suited her. It fell in a fringe over her forehead, and made her eyes look more interesting, less fishy. She had nice clothes on, too—a brand new coat with a fur collar, as good as Anita's any day. And when she took it off, as she was doing now, she had a new green sweater and a plaid skirt, clean white knee-length socks and new brown shoes—shoes that fitted.

"Coo! Don't she look nice?" breathed Anita. "Who's that lady with her?"

"She's from the welfare, I think," whispered Janet. "I seen her before."

"We'll see what we can do, eh Josie?" Miss Lawson was saying. "Now I think you'd better be a boy, with your nice short hair, so you can keep that sweater on and we'll find a pair of trousers——" She was rummaging through a pile of dressing-up clothes on the floor beside her desk. "Here we are, just the thing!" She held up some ragged black trousers. "Put them on—here, Anita, help Josie to put these on." She turned back to the welfare lady. "Well, if she doesn't sing, it doesn't matter, she'll have been on stage with the rest of them. Thank you for bringing her. I think she'll be all right now, if you'd like to join the audience." The welfare lady smiled her thanks and went out.

Anita noticed a big bruise on the side of Josie's face. She felt shy and awkward with her. Did Josie remember all the hateful things she, Anita, had shouted at her when they had last seen each other? Did Josie blame Anita because her dad had caught her and given her a hiding? She felt she was to blame, but she didn't know what to say. Then Jackie came up. "Josie," she said, "I'm—I'm glad you're better—and—and—I'm sorry——"

"I'm sorry, too," said Anita, quickly, "I'm sorry for shouting at you. I didn't mean it, and I'm going to ask my mum if you can come to my firework party."

Josie looked at them both, and then smiled suddenly. "It's all right," she said, "you'll go on being friends with me, won't you? I'm going to sing in the concert tonight, and then I'm going home to my gran's to live, but I'm still going to come to this school. I'm going to come every day, too. My gran don't live near the block so Larry O'Dare can't chase me no more." It was the longest speech they had ever heard Josie make.

When the time came for the operetta, and the peasant music was played, the three friends moved on to the stage among the strangely dressed crowd. They performed the actions—Josie copying the other two—of carrying heavy loads and digging, then hiding from the soldiers who came tramping on. All this went well, except that Jackie knelt on Anita's skirt when they were hiding, and when they all jumped up again to sing their song, Anita was one of the first. There was a horrible tearing sound, and Jackie, still kneeling on the floor, covered her mouth with her hands, gazing horrified at the great hole in the brown skirt. Anita clutched it to her angrily, and some people in the audience sniggered. Miss Roberts in the wings was waving her arms to tell Anita to go on as if nothing had happened. The children were all moving round to make a big semi-circle, and Miss Lawson at the piano was playing the opening bars of their song. Just in time Anita remembered about the audience, and hobbled into her place in the semi-circle.

Everyone began to sing. They had three verses to sing altogether, and then came Josie's verse, then Marissa had her verse, and everyone sang the last verse. They were all rather nervous. Miss Roberts waved her arms frantically to get them to sing up, and Miss Lawson kept looking over the top of the piano, and wriggling her eyebrows.

Then it was Josie's turn. The children all looked at her, and Miss Lawson played a note, and nodded to Josie to begin. There was a pause. Jackie saw Josie's face. It was white, and she was licking her lips nervously.

"Come on, Josie," she whispered. Miss Lawson

played Josie's note again. Everyone was breathless. "She's not going to start," thought Jackie. "Oh, please! She've got to." There was only one thing to be done, Jackie took a deep breath, and began to sing it herself in a rather quavery voice, a little off key.

"My home is far across the sea . . ."

For an awful moment she thought Josie was not going to join in, then suddenly it came, strong and tuneful, a little hoarse at first, but getting clearer and more confident with every word. Jackie dropped out, thankfully, and Josie went on singing till the end of the verse. After that she stood rigidly, staring in front of her, as if in astonishment at what she'd done. When it was time for the peasants to go off the stage, Anita had to push her.

"I never thought she was going to do it! Honest!" said Jackie. She felt so relieved she couldn't stop talking and laughing once they were back in the classroom. "I thought I was going to have to sing the solo instead."

"Then the audience wouldn't have clapped like that!" said Anita.

"You was good, Jackie," said Sharon suddenly, coming up to them in her nurse's clothes. "She wouldn't have done it without you." She dashed off, as it was her turn to be on stage.

Marissa said to Josie, "I thought you sang lovely—better than me."

Some of the boy peasants came up.

"Cor—didn't think you'd do it, Josie."

"You was ever so good."

"Do you have lessons for your voice, an' that?" enquired Paul.

147
398
4
1592
DONALD GREY

"No," said Josie, never having heard of such things. "I don't think so."

"You ought to," they said.

"Garn—she don't need 'em," said Steven.

Josie stood among the group of children. She said hardly anything, but her cheeks were glowing, and her eyes were sparkling, and now at last she was really one of them.

It was happiness and safety—the kind of feeling she'd known when she was in the hide-out. She wouldn't be able to go into the hide-out any more—they were putting spikes and broken glass on the wall. But she didn't need it now.

THE END